Fantasy and Reconciliation

Recent Titles in Contributions in Women's Studies

Fantasy and Reconciliation

Contemporary Formulas of Women's Romance Fiction

Kay Mussell

Contributions in Women's Studies, Number 46

9952

GREENWOOD PRESS
WESTPORT, CONNECTICUT · LONDON, ENGLAND

Library of Congress Cataloging in Publication Data

Mussell, Kay.
    Fantasy and reconciliation.

    (Contributions in women's studies, ISSN 0147-104X ;
no. 46)
    Bibliography: p.
    Includes index.
    1. Women in literature.   2. American fiction—Women
authors—History and criticism.   3. English fiction—
Women authors—History and criticism.   4. American
fiction—20th century—History and criticism.
5. English fiction—20th century—History and
criticism.   6. Love stories, American—History and
criticism.   7. Love stories, English—History and
criticism.   I. Title.   II. Series.   III. Title: Romance
fiction.
PS374.W6M79   1984   813'.54'09352042   83-12731
ISBN 0-313-23915-0 (lib. bdg.)

Library of Congress Catalog Card Number: 83-12731
ISBN: 0-313-23915-0
ISSN: 0147-104X

First published in 1984

Greenwood Press
A division of Congressional Information Service, Inc.
88 Post Road West
Westport, Connecticut 06881

Printed in the United States of America

10 9 8 7 6 5 4 3 2 1

For Boris and to Sarah and Megan

Man's love is of man's life a thing apart
'Tis a woman's whole existence.

George Gordon, Lord Byron

Did you ever see a happy woman in your life? Of
course, I do not mean a girl—like Priscilla, and
a thousand others, for they are all alike, while
on the sunny side of experience—but a grown
woman. How can she be happy, after discovering
that fate has assigned her but one single event,
which she must contrive to make the substance
of her whole life? A man has his choice of innumerable events.

Zenobia in Nathaniel Hawthorne's
The Blithedale Romance

Contents

Preface

I first became interested in romances and romance readers in the mid–1960s when I asked a group of high school juniors why they liked to read novels by Mary Stewart, Phyllis Whitney, Victoria Holt, and Georgette Heyer. When they replied that their mothers and older sisters recommended romances, I caught my first glimpse of the romance underground: readers who share copies of favorite novels with friends and recommend books and authors to each other. Later, in graduate school, I wrote a paper on the modern gothic romance formula, contrasting it with the gothic novels of the eighteenth and nineteenth centuries. That paper, much expanded, became my dissertation, "The World of Modern Gothic Fiction: American Women and Their Social Myths."

While I worked on my dissertation, the contemporary women's movement began to influence scholarship and led to a new academic interest in women's studies. In every field, researchers began to study the experience of women, but romances and feminist scholarship have little in common. Romances rarely challenge the social order, and they do not urge women to recognize oppression or to revolt; instead, they reinforce the value of traditional roles in a changing society. Somehow, it didn't seem to fit. John Cawelti wrote in 1976:

There seems little doubt that most modern romance formulas are affirmations of the ideal of monogamous marriage and feminine domesticity. No doubt the coming age of women's liberation will invent significantly new formulas for romance, if it does not lead to the total rejection of the moral fantasy of love triumphant.[1]

But readers have not rejected the romance fantasy; for despite significant changes in the life-styles of American women, romances sell more widely now than in 1960 when Gerald Gross of Ace Books coined the term *gothic* to describe a new paperback series of women's mysteries.[2] Romance formulas exhibit astonishing resilience and flexibility over time, most recently in the accommodations of romance publishers to feminism and the sexual revolution. Although gothics sell less widely today, romances remain popular, most notably in the two dominant formulas of the 1970s: erotic and series romances. Some recent romances feature women with career commitments and sexual experience, but the essential characteristics of romances remain constant, even though the relative popularity of specific formulas may have shifted.

All romances take place in a similar fictional world. The essential assumptions of romance formulas—belief in the primacy of love in a woman's life, female passivity in romantic relationships, support for monogamy in marriage, reinforcement of domestic values—have not faded or significantly altered. How can such apparently conservative and traditional stories be especially popular today, when we see many women casting off old roles and values and choosing to live more instrumental lives in the world? This book addresses that paradox.

Although I have read many hundreds of romances, this study will not deal with all or even with a large number. I have chosen to concentrate on a few major authors within each formula, and I have limited discussion to key works by those authors. For the series romance, I cite more authors than in the other formulas because of the tighter publisher control over content, significant recent formulaic variations, and proliferation of new series. Janet Dailey and Charlotte Lamb write for both Harlequin and Silhouette, and both are popular writers of the traditional series formula. Amii Lorin (Candlelight), Brooke Hastings (Silhouette), and Karen van der Zee (Harlequin) exemplify the new series romance.

For erotic romances with historical settings, I use Rosemary Rogers, an early and popular writer in the formula. For contemporary erotics, my examples include Janet Dailey and

Danielle Steel. In the romantic mystery formulas, Mary Stewart represents novels of romantic suspense, while Victoria Holt [pseudonym for Eleanor Burford Hibbert] and Phyllis Whitney exemplify the more domestic gothic romance. For Stewart, most examples come from *Nine Coaches Waiting* or *My Brother Michael*. For Holt, I use *Bride of Pendorric* and *Mistress of Mellyn*.

Romantic biographies are represented by Roberta Gellis, Anya Seton, and Jean Plaidy [also a pseudonym for Eleanor Burford Hibbert], with Seton's *Katherine* providing most examples. Historical romances depict many eras of human (female) history, but here I restrict discussion to a popular recent version, the Regency romance as invented by Georgette Heyer. Selected novels include Heyer's *Sylvester, or the Wicked Uncle* and *Frederica*; Barbara Cartland's Regency romances provide a few examples.

In letting the part stand for the whole, I am specifically recognizing that a literary formula presents a coherent vision of the world to readers and that a detailed reading of a few of the most important or influential novels can elucidate the mass of books beneath the surface. In addition, I recognize that, at times, this material does not lend itself to straightforward treatment. Romances span a range from the laughable to the skillful or clever. My own prejudices and biases will obviously show, so I will make them clear at the outset, both in preference and in approach.

The most interesting romance writers of the past thirty years are Mary Stewart, Georgette Heyer, and Anya Seton because these three writers rarely succumb to the most limiting formulaic conventions. Mary Stewart's originality derives from her delineation of complex settings and character types, her use of a wide range of literary models, and her graceful and stylish prose. Georgette Heyer, while working in a limited field—the Regency romance—has nevertheless made it her own; virtually every Regency writer covets the accolade "in the tradition of Georgette Heyer."[3] Her heroines are appealing and spunky; her men, vulnerable and tender. Her wit and humor, if not up to the standard of her inspiration, Jane Austen—and who could write so well?—is at least crisp, pointed, and origi-

nal. Anya Seton specializes in thoroughly researched historical novels about women, and she has written many fewer books
than most other romance authors because of her careful preparation for each book. She chooses a different historical period
for each novel, and she makes it live.

In approach I am a feminist, although one word is inadequate to define the vantage point from which I examine these
books. Feminism represents, I believe, a complex configura-
tion of values and positions, skeptical and subversive of the
status quo but also conservative in intent, for it aims to conserve the abilities and choices of women in culture. My feminism, however, does not lead me to reject broadly humanistic
values or to downgrade men or to push all women into a new
and active role in the world. Instead, I want to question the
way things are by pointing to paradoxical options and values
for women in contemporary American culture. I find no particularly inherent conflict (other than lack of time) among my
roles as wife, mother, teacher, and writer; but I recognize that
perhaps the major achievement of the women's movement lies
in its influence on women who might feel such a conflict.

Our socialization encourages us to feel guilty when we do
not perform like super-people, especially if we choose to work
outside the home. The women's movement may not have eased
our guilt; but we are more aware now of our right to be treated
individually instead of as members of a stereotyped group, and
feminism has given us a limited freedom to *choose* our roles.
The traditional, automatic choice between family and career,
however, has given way to an equally problematic imperative
to have it all and to a new orthodoxy that devalues women's
traditional roles and functions.

I write from the perspective of one who believes that women
do not have to fall for the obvious or define their lives by the
quality of the relationship they may or may not have with a
man. I write, however, as a woman who finds it impossible to
denigrate those who make choices different from mine and as
one who understands with empathy the attractions of a life as
wife, mother, and homemaker. That life was not and is not my
only choice, and yet I think I understand the attraction of a
fictional fantasy that celebrates the domestic values the wom-

en's movement has set out to change. This book does not defend romances—either as art or as appropriate models for female lives—but I hope it respects, understands, and thus defends those women who choose to read them.

In a sense, this book examines the underside of the women's movement and, perhaps, one of its inevitable results. The pressures of women's liberation cause many reactions. For some, it frees us to imagine a new and wider vision of the possibilities open to us. But for other women, the movement poses a threat, for it promises to call into question the very basis of decisions made years ago that are difficult to revoke. Why else would some women be so militant about the value of their traditional roles if they did not feel severely threatened by an apparently massive attack on the worth of their lives?

Many feminists seem equally threatened by the widespread popularity of romances, since the world posited and the values reinforced appear to be inimical to their most cherished ideals of women acting and living in a wider sphere. I cannot, however, condemn romances as enemies of women, because I believe they raise meaningful issues and espouse real values for many women. Although the characters in these books make choices we feminists prefer to reject, heroines face dilemmas in fiction that all women confront, consciously or unconsciously, in daily life. John Cawelti describes romances as fantasies of the "all-sufficiency of love"—a felicitous phrase.[4] We may not believe that love is all-sufficient—I certainly do not—but we make a mistake if we then assume that love is irrelevant or subversive of our lives or a trap. We cannot totally reject the hegemony of the traditional domestic and nurturing roles, for most of us belong to families while we try to work out our destinies as individuals.

From that truth derives my greatest debt: to my family. Without the examples of the women who came before me—my grandmother, my mother and aunts, my cousins—I would never have come to these conclusions or begun to write this book. For the women in my family, marriage did not exclude careers, even if they worked part-time or after the children could begin to care for themselves. Few of my relatives defined themselves as career women; that attitude came to fruition in my own generation. But each showed me, in the relation between their work histories and their family values, that simple questions could have complex answers.

Role models I had, but my primary encouragement came from my father, who never gave me a hint that I should settle for the obvious or should subordinate my intellectual life to a more domestic one. He encouraged me, challenged me, and cared about my decisions; and he provided a wealth of intellectual stimulation, good conversation, and loving tolerance as I made the decisions that gradually led me to a realistic assessment of who I was and what I wanted from my life.

Others also deserve my gratitude. I wrote my first paper on romances for John Cawelti, and he encouraged me to continue the study. Robert A. Corrigan directed my dissertation and helped me sort out an apparently impossible welter of material. My students at The American University never let me get away with an easy generalization, and they asked the toughest questions: "How can you, as a feminist, find anything positive to say about romances?" The National Endowment for the Humanities provided support for two crucial months of research at the Library of Congress.

My daughters, Sarah and Megan, remind me every day of the power of sexism. ("The boys won't let me pick up worms with them 'cause I'm a girl.") And my husband, Boris Weintraub, insisted in a gracious way that I stop gathering research and get down to writing. During the years he has lived with this book, he has tolerated my dragging books and note cards along on vacations, encouraged me to take off summers and a sabbatical year to write, driven miles out of our way on unfamiliar and narrow English roads to track down just one more piece of information on an obscure novel, and been the best live-in editor anyone could want.

Finally, some friends showed me daily over a period of years what it could mean to live fully and joyfully as a woman: Mary, Renee, Stephanie, Meg, Gay, Aggie, Linda, Susan, Margaret, Sherry, Laura, Debbie, Brett, Tracy, Roberta, Ricki, Ann, Valerie, Cricket, Claire, Jo, Janet, Doris, and many more. You know who you are and I thank you.

Notes

1. John G. Cawelti, *Adventure, Mystery, and Romance: Formula Stories as Art and Popular Culture* (Chicago: Univ. of Chicago Press, 1976), 42.

2. Phyllis A. Whitney, "Writing the Gothic Novel," *The Writer* 80 (February 1967): 11.

3. Barbara Cartland, *The Innocent Heiress* (New York: Pyramid, 1950, repr. 1970), front cover.

4. Cawelti, *Adventure, Mystery, and Romance*, 42.

Acknowledgments

Sections of this book have previously appeared, in earlier form, in "Beautiful and Damned: The Sexual Woman in Modern Gothic Fiction," *Journal of Popular Culture* 9 (Summer 1975); "Gothic Novels," in M. Thomas Inge, ed., *Handbook of American Popular Culture*, Vol. 1 (Westport, Conn.: Greenwood Press, 1978); "Romantic Fiction," in M. Thomas Inge, ed., *Handbook of American Popular Culture*, Vol. 2 (Westport, Conn.: Greenwood Press, 1980); previous two essays revised for M. Thomas Inge, ed., *Concise Histories of American Popular Culture* (Westport, Conn.: Greenwood Press, 1982); " 'But Why Do They Read Those Things?': The Female Audience and the Gothic Novel," in Juliann Fleenor, ed., *The Female Gothic* (Montreal: Eden Press, 1983).

Papers based on this material have been read at meetings of the American Studies Association, Popular Culture Association, Midcontinent American Studies Association, and Mid-Atlantic Chesapeake Popular Culture Association.

A background bibliography on women's romances in a historical context appears in my *Women's Gothic and Romantic Fiction: A Reference Guide* (Westport, Conn.: Greenwood Press, 1981).

Fantasy and
Reconciliation

1

A Context for
Analysis of Romances

If the [literary] cultural perspective remains male, as it
largely has, then female writers must either conform to
it, accept a separate and secondary sphere, or, worst of
all, become shrill and demanding in their protests. In
the first instance, they are accepted as exceptions, honorary members in the male club—which itself extracts
its price in cutting them off from the wellsprings of female experience and criticism. In the second, they sub-
side into peripheral status, drawing strength from the
commitment of their readers, but sacrificing—let us
face it—the demands of the most stringent professional
competition. In the last, and most painfully unfair, they
appear to sin most woefully against prevailing standards: sinning against the disinterested purity of style,
they fall from cultural grace itself.[1]

Elizabeth Fox-Genovese

Romances are escape fantasy. Like other formulas of popular fiction—the detective story, the spy story, the Western,
science fiction—they appeal to particular readers in search of
a specific vicarious experience. Unlike these other formulaic
books, however, romances are with few exceptions written by
women, read by women, and published for women. They have
a long history and wide distribution: generations of readers read

romances in English and other languages. In the last two or three decades, romance formulas have been highly profitable for publishers; they rarely appear on bestseller lists, but individual readers buy and read them in large quantities.[2] Although they are rarely reviewed, they are widely advertised.

Today, romance formulas differ from their eighteenth- and nineteenth-century predecessors because each era finds its own models for the familiar tale; and yet the fictional world they describe remains remarkably unchanged over time. Their sources lie in the mainstream of popular fiction for women since the eighteenth century, developing in a long and almost unbroken line of stories that center on—whatever the other ingredients of the plot—the course and culmination of one woman's love story. The popularity of romances has been cyclical; in some periods, romances are plentiful and in others submerged. Over time, they show changes in plot and character within a flexible range of conventions. For example, today they portray human sexuality more explicitly than in the past, although formulaic assumptions about male sexuality, at least, have not altered as much as one might expect from Samuel Richardson's *Pamela* to one of last month's Harlequin Romances.

Moreover, the distribution of romances increased in the 1970s; and in the past twenty-five years, romance formulas have responded rapidly to alterations in women's experience in culture with formulaic variations that mirror the concerns of readers. Romantic mystery formulas dominated the 1960s, followed by periods of popularity for Regency, erotic, and series romances. In the mid–1970s, the Canadian firm of Harlequin, an affiliate of the British publishing company Mills and Boon, made startling inroads into the paperback fiction market of the United States with series of romances that prompted other companies to emulate Harlequin with new romances of their own. In 1972, Mills and Boon combined with Harlequin to sell 27 million copies worldwide, exclusive of translations; in 1973, they sold more than 30 million; in 1974, more than 40 million.[3] In a 1980 *Publishers Weekly* advertisement, Harlequin claimed sales of over 168-million copies in 1979.[4] A 1981 Harlequin advertisement claimed: "Harlequins are the best sellers in the best selling category of paperbacks: romance. 4 out of every 10 books sold are romances, with Harlequin selling 7 times as many as its closest competitor."[5] Harlequin's competitors, however, have recently reduced the company's market share. In November 1982, Harlequin claimed 58 percent of total sales for series romances, down substantially from its virtual monopoly in the previous decade.[6]

Today, series romances dominate the market but other romance formulas—especially the erotic formulas—continue to do well, as a cursory survey of the fiction shelves of any bookstore or the paperback racks of a public library will attest. Romances written decades ago by popular authors remain in print, frequently in newly packaged series; and new novels by a few well-known writers become bestsellers. In 1982, new mass market paperbacks by Rosemary Rogers and Danielle Steel sold more than two million copies each; a Janet Dailey novel had sales of over one and a half million; and Steel, Laurie McBain, Jennifer Wilde, Valerie Sherwood, and Phyllis Whitney each had a book with sales of more than one million copies. On the trade paperback lists, the top-selling novel was Kathleen Woodiwiss's *A Rose in Winter*, a book published late in the year that nevertheless outsold all others for a total of 1,800,000 copies. Other bestselling romance authors in trade paperback editions included Janet Dailey, Danielle Steel, and Patricia Matthews.[7]

Recent success has led to increasing visibility for the romance field. In 1981, authors met in the first annual convention of the Romance Writers of America, a group that distributes a monthly newsletter featuring information on marketing, publishing, and writers. The RWA and other organizations hold workshops and meetings for both published and aspiring writers. Publications for romance readers offer recommendations on books and information on authors, and how-to-write-a-romance books proliferate. In 1983, *Publishers Weekly* announced six new romance series: Harlequin American Romances, Bantam's Loveswept Romances, Avon's Finding Mr. Right, New American Library's Rapture Romances, Silhouette's Intimate Moments, and Jove's To Have and To Hold Romances.[8]

Despite their broad distribution and popularity, however, romances remain misunderstood because they are read by a largely inarticulate audience that lacks access to outlets of opinion and expression. In addition, the story these books tell—love, courtship, marriage—frequently lacks the adventurous action of other popular formulas, for the drama of romances occurs in a small, enclosed, interior space, in a domestic circle with a limited number of characters, narrated from the perspective of the major female character. Romances are primarily concerned with the process of mate selection and, secondarily, with those domestic activities—nurturing and homemaking—traditionally assigned to women in Western culture. They mirror the assumptions of Lord Byron in his felicitous phrase: "Man's love is of man's life, a thing apart/'Tis a woman's whole existence."

One does not have to agree with Byron's assessment to recognize its relevance to the reading choices of some women. In romance formulas—unlike those fantasy patterns that appeal primarily to men—protagonists do not usually recur, like James Bond, from book to book. Once a woman's love story has been told, repetition of the experience for her is inappropriate—repetition would, in fact, undermine the entire premise of her story—and her life is, for dramatic purposes, over. Romances suggest that the greatest adventure for a woman occurs when she finds the one man with whom she will share the rest of her life. If a heroine returned for a repeat performance, her first love story would be devalued, because she would have made a mistake the first time around.

Because romances are published in a cheap and disposable format, few individual novels survive over time. Some available catalogues of nineteenth-century booksellers and a few documents of antiquarian scholarship reveal the outlines, but many of the original novels are currently unavailable in any form. Today, Harlequin and Silhouette, the leading series publishers, issue about twenty titles per month each; and individual readers can only sample the range. Romance conventions, however, have influenced serious writers for generations; and a measure of the persistence and flexibility of the formulas can be found in the use of romance conventions in novels by authors whose work has been systematically preserved and studied.

Jane Austen, for example, wrote in *Northanger Abbey* a clever satire on gothic romances in her day; and she has also been cited as a source for the contemporary Regency romance. In *Jane Eyre*, Charlotte Brontë used the outlines of popular romance in creating her masterpiece of woman's consciousness; that book, in turn, provided a durable model for writers of contemporary gothic romances. Nathaniel Hawthorne, writing to his publisher, excoriated his rival novelists: "America is now wholly given over to a d——d mob of scribbling women, and I should have no chance of success while the public taste is occupied with their trash—and should be ashamed of myself if I did."[9] And yet Hawthorne's *The Scarlet Letter*, as a historical romance with a female protagonist whose conflict with her society begins with a sexual indiscretion, derives partially from romance conventions. In addition, its publication followed scores of romances by nineteenth-century authors who wrote about the plight of women in the patriarchy of colonial New England.[10] In *The Turn of the Screw*, Henry James used a romance convention by having his protagonist tell her own story, which begins as if it would be one more of those classic tales of an insignificant governess who wins the love of her powerful employer. More recently, Margaret Atwood's *Lady Oracle* features a woman who secretly writes costume gothics; the novel plays off the narrative of her life against the conventions of romance. These and other serious writers—such as Gustave Flaubert, Leo Tolstoy, and Edith Wharton—drew on romance conventions but constructed narratives that both transcended romances and commented on them.

Formula romances, however, use conventions straightforwardly, without irony, in a familiar manner that affords the reader a repeatable vicarious experience. Although individual novels within a formula or group of related formulas may vary in plot, setting, time period, problems, and solutions, the premises of the fictional world—the way it operates, the character relationships, the value system, and the moral imperatives—link disparate novels together. Readers choose formula books because they know they will have a predictable vicarious experience and that the author will not change the rules in midstream. In other words, readers know that a certain moral order will be imposed on experience, that everything will work out according to a predictable value system, and that the vicarious pleasure can be repeated by picking up another book of the same type. Romance readers know the action of the story will be largely controlled by the developing love relationship between hero and heroine; the adventure will derive from the conflicts between potential lovers as they overcome obstacles to their union, and if the woman behaves correctly, she will earn the right to a happy marriage and a satisfying domestic life.

Contemporary romance formulas date at least to the beginning of mature, sustained prose fiction in the English language; Samuel Richardson's *Pamela*, often cited as the first British novel, delineated the outlines of the modern romance. *Pamela* was the first example of the seduction story, a cautionary tale prevalent from the publication of Richardson's novel until the first quarter of the nineteenth century. The seduction story told a simple tale with two possible plots: the young woman resisted the blandishments of a rake, he yielded to her superior virtue, and she earned his love and an offer of marriage; or she yielded her virtue prematurely (before she had his wedding ring on her finger) and then died an ignominious and instructive death. *Pamela* exemplifies, in two long epistolary volumes, the first plot type; and Susanna Haswell Rowson's *Charlotte Temple* illustrates the second. These two versions of the same story were repeated over and over; and, like many other forms of prose fiction, their original British versions were copied by American authors.

Seduction stories established and elaborated several significant romance conventions. The books dramatized the conflicts of young women, presented by life with few respectable options for their adult lives, as they react to the sexual advances of experienced and often ignoble men. The primary conflict in romances derives from an adversarial relationship between male and female characters. Men try to get everything they can without giving anything in return, while women hold out for marriage and respectability. Men have more power and experience than women, and they live under fewer imperatives for sexual self-control. An attempted seduction—as implied by Byron—plays only a minor part in a man's life, but it occupies a central and crucial place in a woman's. If the man succeeds in seducing her, his punishment—if any—is guilt; if she gives in, she may face ostracism or death. On the other hand, if she resists long enough, romances hold out the possibility that the rake will see the error of his ways and go straight, offering marriage and recognizing her as his redeemer from a dissolute and meaningless life. Although the modern romance portrays the battle of the sexes—and female sexuality—in a more contemporary form, the adversarial relationship remains constant; and women continue to risk more severe social sanctions than do men if they fail to acknowledge the prescriptions of the double standard.

The pure seduction story outlived its relevance early in the nineteenth century, when it was superseded in the popular taste by the gothic novels of Horace Walpole, Ann Radcliffe, Matthew Gregory "Monk" Lewis, and their imitators. Gothic novels intensify the implied threat of the seduction story as villains manipulate "actual" or apparent supernatural terrors to seduce or threaten innocent young heroines. As the gothic vogue waned, nineteenth-century romances turned to more mundane, domestic issues, exploring the range of proper female behavior and identity in the work of such now-forgotten authors as Maria Jane McIntosh, Maria Susanna Cummins, and others. From the second quarter of the century through the Civil War, romances were dominated by domestic dramas that defined and defended the female virtues of "purity, piety, domesticity, and submissiveness" for a wide audience of women.[11] During and after the popularity of domestic romances, the tale of gothic adventure continued in the work of such writers as Mrs. E.D.E.N. Southworth, whose heroines faced dangerous dilemmas and behaved with spunk and aggressiveness. By the late nineteenth and early twentieth centuries, these books gave way to a varied group including the historical novels of Mary Johnston, the mysteries and romances of Mary Roberts Rinehart, and the domestic stories of Kathleen Norris. After World War I, some romance authors still popular today began writing in England. During the 1920s, for example, Georgette Heyer and Barbara Cartland, whose Regency romances became popular in the United States in the mid–1960s, published their first books. Daphne du Maurier's *Rebecca*, the first of the modern gothic romances, appeared in 1938.

Contemporary romance formulas came to prominence about 1960, the year in which Eleanor Burford Hibbert issued her first gothic romance, *Mistress of Mellyn*, under the pseudonym Victoria Holt. The reception of this book by readers encouraged writers and publishers alike to emulate its success; and for most of the ensuing decade, new and experienced writers found an eager audience for romantic mysteries with female protagonists. Victoria Holt, of course, did not invent the gothic formula; but her novel, with its close similarities to both *Jane Eyre* and *Rebecca*, restructured and validated the formula for a new generation of readers. Many successful authors of the next few years had written romances before 1960—Mary Stewart, Phyllis Whitney, and Anya Seton, to name a few— but only after the publication of *Mistress of Mellyn*, when publishers sensed the potential new market for romances, did these experienced writers achieve their greatest success. Editors, eager to find new material, encouraged writers to emulate Stewart, Holt, Whitney, Seton, Heyer, and Cartland by reissuing romances originally published decades before. Many were from England, the source of most romance formulas; and the reprinting of older books in a cheap format sparked another wave of imitation by British and American authors.

A significant change in contemporary romance formulas occurred in the early 1970s with the publication of the first books by Rosemary Rogers, Lolah Burford, and Kathleen Woodiwiss, who represented a new generation of authors with a new version of the romance plot, described by publishers and commentators as "erotic historical romances" or "bodice-rippers." Marked by a more explicit portrayal of sexuality, the first erotic romances had historical settings and adventurous plots. Later in the decade erotic romances with contemporary settings appeared. Authors like Danielle Steel and Janet Dailey, for example, wrote books that explored a wider range of social and sexual behavior than had romances of previous years. Simultaneously, the series romance experienced a new wave of interest, exemplified today by Harlequin and its imitators. Recently, series books have become more sophisticated to compete more effectively with the erotic formulas.

Romance formulas vary and change as the concerns and interests of the reading audience alter, but all romances share a common perspective. The narrative unfolds from a woman's point of view; if the heroine does not tell her own story in the first person, the author filters the tale through her perspective. When an author offers a glimpse into the hero's mind, his thoughts invariably center on the heroine and their relationship rather than on other aspects of his experience. In all romances, the love story is the central action and the most significant motivating force. All romances dramatize traditional women's concerns in an atmosphere of exquisite suspense, where mundane events take on an inflated significance. They assert and reinforce a woman's desire to identify and marry the one right man who will remain hers for the rest of her life.

Providing both adventure and romance, they lift readers out of their everyday and open-ended world into a renewable fantasy with a secure and solid beginning, middle, and ending. They offer escape, as does all entertainment, from the frustrations of everyday life; but, more significantly, popular formulas control and manage for readers those problems and frustrations they may sense only unconsciously in daily life. All fiction provides *escape from* present reality; the choice of formula allows *escape to* a world that appears more satisfactory than the readers' own. Formula books appeal to readers because they have this dual function, and readers choose to be entertained by particular formulas that address their specific problems and situations. The formulas of romance confront the concerns of many women in culture, and, as they do, their outlines partially illuminate women's socialization and experience.

Who Reads Romances?

Analysis of formulas should be grounded in examination of their readers, but reliable and thorough information is difficult to obtain and interpret. Readership studies are rare, and most readers are inarticulate about their reading preferences and their reasons for enjoying such pleasures. Romance readers, especially, seem apologetic and occasionally secretive about the books they read, because romances have a reputation as a debased and insignificant literary formula. Romance publishers collect data for use in marketing, but they are understandably stingy in disseminating it because of the intense competition among editors and companies.

Evidence about the readership for romances derives from two main sources: abundant impressionistic information based on marketing and distribution techniques and a few surveys that are more suggestive than definitive. Romances are distributed in places frequented by women: grocery stores, drug stores, suburban bookstores, and public libraries. Most television advertising appears during the daytime hours—during game shows and soap operas—and occasionally during prime-time shows that might draw an audience predisposed to read romances. Harlequin, for example, advertised during a television showing of *Gone With the Wind* in 1979 and coverage of the royal wedding in 1981.

No doubt, the vast majority of romance readers are female, but little information on male readers currently exists. *Boy Meets Girl*, a romance newsletter, suggests that men constitute about 1 or 2 percent of twenty-two million romance readers.[12] However, the figure may understate the proportion because men have reasons even stronger than those of women to hide an addiction to the romance fantasy. Using female pseudonyms, a few male writers have achieved success writing romances, especially in the more erotic formulas (for example, Tom E. Huff [Jennifer Wilde] and Bill Lambert [Willa Lambert]).[13]

The common stereotype of romance readers suggests that only maladjusted women could find the fantasy attractive. Some commentators assume that romance readers are either teen-aged girls, bored housewives, or frustrated spinsters. Why else, the question seems to go, would a woman spend significant amounts of time and money reading and re-reading the same simple, highly unrealistic tale? But the fragmentary statistical evidence suggests, instead, that readers of romances represent a heterogeneous cross section of well-adjusted, literate, and normal women who include the reading of romances in the span of their everyday activities.[14] Reading of romances does not seem to crowd out other pursuits—even other types of reading—nor does it lead to a reduction in face-to-face encounters with others.[15] No evidence indicates romances directly harm readers, and the sheer number of readers tends to refute easy assumptions that only unrealistic or frustrated women read them.

Romance readers range from teenagers to senior citizens, include both employed women and housewives, and cut across socioeconomic and education levels. Jan Hajda's survey of women in Baltimore found that many readers cited among their preferences historical novels, love stories, suspense and biographical novels—all well within the range of romance formulas.[16] Hajda reported that the women who read (as opposed to those who did not) had many more social contacts and were more active in a variety of pursuits. His evidence suggests that reading, for these women, was less a way of retreating from reality than of expanding the range of their experience through fiction. Making a distinction between solitude (a chosen, rejuvenating condition) and loneliness (an involuntary and painful state), he concluded:

More or less avid book reading, as described here, seems to be riding a paradox. The desire to read is associated both with gregariousness and with opportunity and desire for solitude. The act of book reading simultaneously requires a fair degree of social integration and of individual autonomy. Reading deepens contact with humanity, rather than drawing away from it.[17]

Hajda's conclusions about his subjects were reinforced by a 1978 survey on book reading in the United States. The researchers who compiled the Yankelovich, Skelly, and White study for the Book Industry Study Group stated: "Book readers, and particularly heavier volume ones, are *not* solitary people. They have the greatest involvement in other leisure time activities."[18] Interviewing a cross section of the American adult population correlated with census data, the authors found that average book readers are women, white, well educated, affluent, and under fifty.[19] Surprisingly, they watch as much television as those who do not read books.[20] Among women readers, "the presence of minor children in the home appears to be a 'plus' in favor of book reading";[21] and childless employed women read books in a higher proportion than childless housewives.[22] Women as a group report that they read for leisure and pleasure, and they read more novels than do men.[23]

The Yankelovich survey divided reading choices into categories and included romances in the tabulations of data. The survey notes that these books are read and purchased in exceptionally large numbers by individual readers.[24] *Publishers Weekly* reports the same trend in its new series on book distribution, conducted by the Gallup polling organization. The survey divided readers into preference categories that show romance buyers selecting books more for the "appeal of the book itself" than from advertisements or recommendations of bookstore employees. Romance buyers pay little attention to reviews or book clubs but rely heavily on recommendations from friends.[25] Unless one assumes romance readers belong to a large, frustrated, solitary, overimaginative, uneducated, and leisured group of spinsters, this information does not correlate with stereotypical assumptions.

Data about romance reading in Britain appears in two older surveys performed by sociologist Peter Mann for the firm of Mills and Boon, publishers of the most successful international series of romances. Mann surveyed the recipients of the Mills and Boon catalogue and discovered that the readership was substantially more heterogeneous than he and others had assumed. The majority of respondents were married women some years older than the average age of courtship and marriage, the constant subject of the novels. Mann also noted a higher-than-expected level of education and occupational prestige among readers.[26] A 1982 market survey conducted by Harlequin indicates that 15 percent of its readership in the United States consists of management-level women earning more than $25,000 per year—about double the figure expected by the firm when it began research.[27] In the decade between the Mann and Harlequin research, Mills and Boon/Harlequin made substantial changes in the formula, including some older and more professional heroines, which might account for part of the unexpected increase in highly educated readers.

Admittedly, these data must be used with caution. Because the Mann survey was sent to a mailing list of devoted readers, it excluded a large portion of the market. The high response rate may have represented a sample of more educated readers who were willing to fill out the form. The survey excluded women who acquire books from the public library, borrow romances from friends, or buy them in bookstores. Respondents in the Harlequin research included about fifty executive women who volunteered to be interviewed by phone when they answered an advertisement in the *New York Times*.

Although the results of the Mann survey are not conclusive and do not include American readers of romances, they indicate the heterogeneous audience for romances. Because the relative age range of readers correlates with the Yankelovich profile of readers in the United States, a substantial number of romance readers must be married women in their middle years. But John Cawelti suggests in *Adventure, Mystery, and Romance* that the most successful formulas of popular fiction maximize the possible range of reader responses to attract a wide and diverse audience. Individuals converge on a single formula or group of formulas because they find elements of appeal that may be similar to, but not identical with, those of other readers.[28]

The range of the readers—in age, economic and educational position, and marital status—supports Cawelti's assumptions about the appeal of formulas to broad groups of readers. He suggests that particular formulas attract readers because they invoke and manage aspects of experience relevant to readers' interests. Romance readers appear to be concerned, for distinct reasons and from diversity of experience, with their relationships with men, that very private bond that so rarely occupies center stage in mainstream fiction. Young women, not yet assigned for life to a mate, might read these books for different reasons than do their mothers or grandmothers. But romances apparently carry a message that many women wish to hear, whether it lies outside their personal experience, contradicts it, or confirms it. That message, repeated from story to story, suggests that a woman's traditional sphere can be both fulfilling and exciting. Through a vicarious and yet ultimately confining set of events, romances reaffirm and heighten the value of those areas of human life that have been most frequently the province of women.

Interpretations of Romances

For many reasons, romances have been devalued and misunderstood throughout their history. Two centuries ago, critics and moralists argued against the proliferation of novels and lending libraries because novels were suspected of corrupting the morals of innocent young girls who were presumed to make up the bulk of the audience. Today, romances are shunned as trivial and attacked as unrealistic and subversive. Disdaining to read them, critics and reviewers have instead been satisfied to relegate them to the garbage heap of fiction—along with that other unfavored literary genre, pornography—in a gesture of contempt that denies the validity of both the books and their readers.

Male readers and male critics frequently ignore or denigrate the romance fantasy because its drama lacks relevance to male socialization patterns. For female readers and critics, however, the issues are more problematic, for romances address tensions and problems of women's experience that are difficult to evade successfully. Most women must, one way or another, consider the implications of the romance fantasy for their own lives, even if they never read romances for pleasure, because romances represent a portion of experience that all women confront.

Three main arguments are advanced against romances, either directly or indirectly, in work by both journalists and scholars. The first attitude, and the simplest, dismisses the novels as trivial and therefore unworthy of attention or comment. Criticizing a film, novel, or television program as a "Harlequin romance" has become an automatic phrase of contempt by reviewers who may never have read a romance. The assumption that romances are unworthy of attention helps to explain why they are so rarely reviewed or accorded serious critical attention. In addition, the attitude may lead to embarrassment for romance readers and writers, who frequently seem apologetic or defensive about their interest in a fantasy that has a reputation for insignificance or simplicity. Describing her odyssey from secretiveness to pride about her work, one romance author reported that her friends expressed open contempt for her "sell out" as a writer. She shared their attitude at first, until she realized publishers would not buy her work unless she wrote carefully and with respect for the formula.[29] This assumption—trivia deserves no serious attention—mirrors the cultural attitude held by many men and women toward the woman's sphere and the female experience.

The second argument, put forth most consistently by feminist critics, charges that romances are subversive of women's lives, for they encourage readers to succumb to stereotypical patterns that pacify and obscure women's legitimate frustrations in the performance of traditional roles. Romances, these critics argue, encourage dependency on men and reinforce female passivity. One writer (male) says:

Frankly, I'm offended by [romances'] depiction of a one-dimensional, insensitive macho hero as the ideal object of a woman's love. And I resent their portrayal of a quivering heroine who is ultimately dependent upon a man's adoration for her sense of personal worth. But mostly I choke on the romanticizing of a relationship that confuses an immature power struggle for love.[30]

No doubt the criticism has validity, but it isolates women's fantasy fiction from its literary and cultural context. Male adventure formulas, for example, reinforce assumptions for men that are no less limiting and unrealistic than those prescribed for women; male formulas also encourage capitulation to cultural norms and relieve readers of the need to reevaluate their life choices and roles. Romances are no more untrue, overwrought, and destructive of human relationships than the popular male fantasies of Ian Fleming and Mickey Spillane, whose heroes frequently treat women with violence or contempt. After James Bond defeats each villain, he receives an explicitly sexual reward when he makes love to a woman he abandons at the end of each book. Only once does he marry her, and his wife dies as they drive away on their honeymoon. Women's fantasies may differ from men's, but they are no less legitimate.

In addition, the writer just cited apparently bases his conclusions on a single romance, a book from a series that shows little influence from changing cultural patterns for women. But female critics also succumb to stereotypical assumptions based on limited reading. In a newspaper article riddled with factual errors, an aspiring romance writer apologized for her ambition (saying she was in it for fun and money) while asserting that romance heroines invariably sacrifice their careers for love, a convention that may have been true in the past but appears less frequently in recent books.[31]

The argument that romances are subversive to women has been leveled at women's books of the past and the present; today, it represents one position in the liveliest debate on romance reading and women's culture. Contemporary critics disagree on the impact of romance formulas on readers. Barbara Welter and Ann Douglas, for example, argue that nineteenth-century domestic romances pacified and enervated their audience by encouraging women to conform, while Nina Baym and Helen Waite Papashvily found in the same novels signs of covert revolt and models for development of an autonomous female self.[32] Occupying the middle ground between these two positions, Mary Kelley argues that nineteenth-century romances represent a conflict between the authors' intention and the novels' covert message for readers.[33]

These critical disagreements have counterparts in commentary on contemporary romance novels. Joanna Russ asserts that modern gothic romances

are a direct expression of the traditional feminine situation (at least a middle-class feminine situation) and that they provide precisely the kind of escape reading a middle-class believer in the feminine mystique needs, without involving elements that either go beyond the feminine mystique or would be considered immoral in its terms.[34]

She describes the gothic heroine as an inactive character who plays the part of a victim. "Most striking about these novels is the combination of intrigue, crime, and danger with the Heroine's complete passivity."[35]

Janice Radway, however, finds substantial evidence of independence and self-assertiveness in gothic heroines, qualities that heroes admire and value when the two protagonists join to solve the mystery. "Female independence," she says, "it would seem, does not threaten men or cause them to retaliate; rather it seduces and transforms them."[36] She believes that "the gothic's central concern is its preoccupation with the proper way to realize female identity."[37]

An examination by Carol Thurston and Barbara Doscher of erotic historical romances ("bodice-rippers") suggests that the books support and reinforce contemporary feminist attitudes about women.

Critics, especially feminist critics, tend to lump all paperback romances together and take great delight in aiming potshots at the archetypal submissive-pure heroine and macho-stud hero or in attacking the whole bunch as soft porn. At the same time they dismiss readers of such drivel as mindless drones living in a fantasy world. But we recently looked at more than fifty erotic historical romances published between 1964 and 1981, and came to a different conclusion.[38]

Thurston and Doscher found heroines who complained vigorously against being categorized as weak and inferior, demanded respect from their lovers, and rejected men who refused to consider their needs. Quoting from their sample of novels and from the statements of contemporary feminists, they argue that erotic historical romances disseminate "feminist" visions to readers who might otherwise resist changing models of womanhood.

Some commentators interpret romances as a way for women to fight back against men. In *Loving with a Vengeance*, Tania Modleski describes series and gothic romances as a covert expression of female rage in protesting women's sense of helplessness in the face of male power and authority. Although she deplores the heroines' eventual capitulation to cultural norms for women, her argument assumes that romances represent a subversive force that allows female concerns to find expression in fiction.[39] Radway suggests that the antagonism between heroes and heroines in the formative stages of the gothic plot "grants the reader license to give free reign [sic] to any pent-up resentment she may feel toward men and to identify with and support a woman who at least initially refuses to be cowed."[40] Like Kelley's analysis of nineteenth-century formulas, Radway's evaluation admits the complexity of romances, for she takes into account the narrative development of the formula rather than concentrating on its static conventions. Consistently, the most convincing analyses of romances are based on the widest reading and pay the greatest attention to the complex dynamic of the romance formula.

The third argument, and the most recent, concerns the novels' portrayal of sexuality, accusing them of idealizing rape or constituting a form of "soft porn" for women. Ann Douglas says: "The Harlequins are porn softened to fit the needs of female emotionality."[41] Another writer suggests "the fantasy confirms a familiar and insidious message: the guy you think is hurting you is really the one who loves you most. This mingling of pain and love, of humiliation and rapture, is a key element in all romance fiction, reinforcing the notion that women are by nature masochistic."[42] Barbara Cartland, a popular writer of Regency romances, concurs, objecting to the increasingly explicit portrayals of sexuality in recent romances: "Images of sex with violence affects the brain . . . and this sex with violence is pandered to by some romantic novels. . . . Some of the new romances have become soft porn, and this is a terrible mistake."[43]

This criticism recognizes explicit sexuality as an important ingredient of romances in recent years. The formula has always found methods to accommodate changing cultural imperatives in its conventions, and the trend toward realism in sexual relationships certainly represents a response to the more permissive sexual behavior of the past decade. But historically all romance formulas portray female sexual responsiveness as the key to identification of the hero, although previous versions describe the experience more obliquely. Despite the less reticent language of contemporary novels, however, sexuality in romances continues to be controlled by assumptions similar to those of the past. Contemporary heroines may not be damned irrevocably for irregular sexual experience, but they frequently suffer for sexual mistakes. Heroes may have a wide range of sexual experience before they commit themselves to a more domestic life, but men who treat heroines as sex objects can never be heroic. Thurston and Doscher, for example, found that the heroines in their sample were not ashamed to admit sexual desire, but they were most attracted to partners who were sensitive and vulnerable. "The central message in the erotic historical romances rings loud and clear: Macho males and saccharine ingenues are the losers in society."[44]

Arguing that romances idealize masochistic tendencies women should not have, these critics concentrate on sexual encounters without reference to either the context of sexuality in romances or its metaphoric role. Heroes may dominate heroines, but never for mere sexual pleasure. Sex scenes dramatize the heroine's acceptance of her repressed erotic impulses, which she can only acknowledge when the hero evokes her sexual feelings. Additionally, designating sexual encounters as rape fantasies limits analysis to the effect of sexual encounters on heroines and minimizes their equally significant impact on heroes. When a hero initiates a heroine sexually, he simultaneously discovers in her an acceptable and fulfilling focus for his passion that assures his future monogamy. Sex in romances is undoubtedly unrealistic, and heroes have significantly more sexual and physical power than heroines; but sex scenes offer a model not for sexual submission but for sexual control. Sexual initiation in romances functions as a significant developmental experience for heroines only in the context of love and commitment.

Actual rape scenes occur rarely in romances, but men pose a constant sexual threat that the fantasy controls in significant ways. If a heroine experiences a violent sexual encounter, her response—and that of the man—carries the metaphoric meaning in the fantasy. In romances, sex unaccompanied by commitment results in pain and degradation, and heroes always understand the distinction between rape and love. If a hero forces a heroine, usually because he assumed she was sexually experienced and treated her without the tenderness he would show to a virgin, he invariably feels shame and guilt. More commonly, the hero dominates the heroine verbally; and if he handles her roughly to prove a point in some scenes, he treats her gently and with respect as the relationship progresses. In the context of the narrative development of romances, satisfying sexual encounters identify appropriate partners who share a commitment to fidelity; and they underscore the patriarchal role of the hero/lover who values the particular qualities of the individual woman he chooses as his wife. In contrast, romances portray actual rape as an act of violence, female subordination, and objectification that heroines fear and resist.

And yet, on the surface, sexual encounters in romances are frequently marked by conflict, arguments, and male authority and control. In *Endless Rapture*, a wide-ranging, idiosyncratic defense of romances and an attack on feminist theory, Helen Hazen asserts that the sexual encounters in romances delineate a natural distinction between the sexes and that female masochism represents a real, nonpathological characteristic of women. Drawing on recent feminist writing on rape and novels written by women, Hazen accuses feminists of misunderstanding both the meaning of rape as an act and the significance of women's fantasies about it. She distinguishes between violent rape (a crime) and fantasy rape (wish fulfillment), arguing that a woman's yearning to be dominated by a sexually potent man arises naturally from biological imperatives. Women bear children and carry on the species, and their urge to reproduce leads to fantasies about sexual expression in a heightened context where a man finds a woman's attractiveness so overwhelming that he cannot control his desire to possess her. Hazen accuses feminists of confusing freedom with masculinity, experience with fantasy, and literature with politics; and she believes the feminist vision will remain a minority view because it misunderstands the "true nature" of women.[45]

The convention of male sexual dominance in romances, however, may have a simpler significance. All fiction requires conflict to maintain suspense, and conflict in romances occurs between hero and heroine as they find their way through the obstacles to romantic fulfillment. No conflict, no plot. Isolating the conflict from its context leads to a misunderstanding of its function. The rape fantasy charge resembles the pervasive belief that violent acts in American society can be explained by counting violent episodes on television programs. Both arguments assume that undesirable social consequences result from undesirable fictional patterns, without distinguishing between wish fulfillment and fear or recognizing that fantasies may be enjoyed on more than one level. Fictional adventures for both men and women set terrifying events at a distance and control natural fears of violation and defeat. No one wants to encounter the shark in *Jaws*, but many people find vicarious reassurance when mere men eliminate the monster. Few men yearn to be James Bond, and yet the audience for Bond novels and films clearly identifies with his superhuman mastery of his precarious world and enjoys the ritualized and objectified control of international terror. Women naturally fear rape and, in responding to the demands of the double standard, they may hesitate to express their sexual desires openly, especially because men traditionally initiate romantic relationships and supposedly "know" more about sex. In making distinctions between varieties of sexual experience, romances manage simultaneously women's fears of powerlessness and desires for fulfillment.

The soft porn argument similarly isolates sex scenes from their metaphoric function by suggesting that sexuality in romances degrades women and portrays them as sex objects. For a heroine, discovery of her sexual nature marks an important step in her adult identity formation. Through her sexual initiation by the hero—consummated or unconsummated—she learns to express herself without fear or embarrassment, and she finds fulfillment only with a man who acknowledges her individual worth. In addition, the argument ignores the historical hegemony of the double standard, the cultural factor that shapes the portrayal of sexuality in romances. Socialization encourages women to desire strong and dominant men, and the fantasy of heroes who control women's sexual expression while capitulating to domestic imperatives both conforms to women's expectations and places a supreme value on women's role in culture. Because cultural inhibitions on female sexuality remain rigid, change may seem simultaneously desirable and disquieting. No doubt, many women find it more acceptable to experience sex vicariously than to express sexual impulses in their actual day-to-day existence.

The evaluation of romances implies a political choice. Those who assume women should be more active in the world at large frequently devalue romances because they do, like other popular formulas, trivialize the genuine problems of human life and present unrealistic options and situations. Critics frequently identify the conservative (undesirable) conventions of romances as harmful to women's right to participate in a wider sphere, for they assume that traditional patterns of female existence lack significance. More significantly, however, in denigrating romances they condemn romance readers for failing to share their own values and commitments, while forgetting that popular art is by nature unrealistic and shallow, and the pleasure derived from formula fiction depends on neither its realism nor its politics.

Understanding romances requires attention to both their narrative development and the cultural context of their readers. Within the range of accepted women's roles and women's stories, romances portray a wide variety of adventures with rich possibilities; and romance formulas celebrate those aspects of female culture ignored most consistently by the culture at large. The patterns of socialization for women have profound psychological consequences that require women to come to terms with the imperatives of femininity before they engage in other kinds of activity. Too many women never make the leap from female to human definition, and they may be unable to leave the insecurities of female definition behind when they move out into the wider world. But romances, like other popular formulas, do not cause the limitations on human life to which they respond.

Romances try to make objective and exciting the subjective models decreed for women, but they do not and cannot move on to autonomous models because those models do not yet exist—in literature or in life. As Joanna Russ points out, existing literary myths are gender specific. With telling examples, she shows how ludicrous it seems to substitute a woman for a man as the protagonist of many archetypal plots, for women exist in fiction in reflected roles that parallel their subsidiary status in culture. Heroines in fiction, she writes, act out "the one occupation of a female protagonist in literature, the one thing she can do, and by God she does it and does it and does it, over and over and over again. She is the protagonist of a Love Story."[46] Fairy tales, serious literature, and romances all share these limitations, for fictional adventure for women occurs conventionally in a specific and limited context that rarely continues after marriage. Unfortunately, no experiences in a woman's life yet contain the imaginative resonance of mate selection, with its complementary heightened world of domesticity and adventure. But blaming romance formulas for the cultural conditions to which they respond only faults the messenger who delivers bad news.

In *Adventure, Mystery, and Romance*, John Cawelti defines four functions common to formula stories. They "affirm existing interests and attitudes by presenting an imaginary world that is aligned with these interests and attitudes"; they "resolve tensions and ambiguities resulting from the conflicting interests of different groups within the culture or from ambiguous attitudes toward particular values"; they "enable the audience to explore in fantasy the boundary between the permitted and the forbidden and to experience in a carefully controlled way the possibility of stepping across this boundary"; and they "assist in the process of assimilating changes in values to traditional imaginative constructs."[47] Because romances perform these same functions for women readers, they delineate important aspects of the values and socialization patterns of their readers and, by extension, provide a valuable source of information about women's lives and experience.

Notes

1. Elizabeth Fox-Genovese, "The New Female Literary Culture," *The Antioch Review* 38 (Spring 1980): 194.

2. Yankelovich, Skelly, and White, Inc., *Consumer Research Study on Reading and Book Purchasing* (Darien, Conn.: The Group, 1978), 137.

3. Peter H. Mann, *A New Survey: The Facts About Romantic Fiction* (London: Mills and Boon, 1974), 5.

4. Advertisement, *Publishers Weekly* (14 April 1980): 26–27.

5. Advertisement, *Publishers Weekly* (17 July 1981): 17.

6. Advertisement, *Publishers Weekly* (26 November 1982): 3.

7. Sally A. Lodge, "Paperback Top Sellers," *Publishers Weekly* (11 March 1983): 37–41.

8. Daisy Maryles and Allene Symons, "Love Springs Eternal: Six New Sensual Romance Lines Coming in '83," *Publishers Weekly* (14 January 1983): 53–58.

9. Nathaniel Hawthorne, quoted in Herbert Ross Brown, *The Sentimental Novel in America* (Durham, N.C.: Duke Univ. Press, 1940), 179.

10. Michael Davitt Bell, *Hawthorne and the Historical Romance of New England* (Princeton, N.J.: Princeton Univ. Press, 1971).

11. Barbara Welter, "The Cult of True Womanhood," *American Quarterly* 18 (Summer 1966): 151–74.

12. Charles Storch, "Female Execs Finding Room for Romances, Publisher Finds," *Chicago Tribune* Business section (30 January 1983): 1.

13. Kathryn Falk, *How to Write a Romance and Get It Published* (New York: Crown, 1983), 262.

14. Jan Hajda, "A Time for Reading," *Trans-Action* 4 (June 1967): 45.

15. Hajda, "A Time for Reading"; also Yankelovich, Skelly, and White, Inc., *Consumer Research Study on Reading*.

16. Hajda, "A Time for Reading."

17. Ibid., 50.

18. Yankelovich, Skelly, and White, Inc., *Consumer Research Study on Reading*, 20.

19. Ibid., 71.

20. Ibid., 28.

21. Ibid., 52.

22. Ibid., 51.

23. Ibid., 79.

24. Ibid., 137, 143.

25. Leonard A. Wood, "Gallup Survey: Nearly 1 in 5 Adult Americans Bought a Book in Early December," *Publishers Weekly* (28 January 1983): 46.

26. Peter H. Mann, *The Romantic Novel: A Survey of Reading Habits* (London: Mills and Boon, 1969), 6.

27. Storch, "Female Execs Finding Room," 1.

28. John G. Cawelti, *Adventure, Mystery, and Romance: Formula Stories as Art and Popular Culture* (Chicago: Univ. of Chicago Press, 1976), 30.

29. Lee Fleming, "True Confessions of a Romance Novelist," *Washington Post Magazine* (5 December 1982): 35–39.

30. Scarff Downing, "A Man's View of Romance Novels," *Network* 1 (January 1983): 7.

31. Lindley Mercer, "Passion to Write," *Washington Post* (18 April 1983): C5.

32. See Welter, "Cult of True Womanhood"; Ann Douglas, *The Feminization of American Culture* (New York: Alfred A. Knopf, 1978); Helen Waite Papashvily, *All the Happy Endings* (New York: Harper, 1956); Nina Baym, *Woman's Fiction: A Guide to Novels by and about Women in America, 1820–1870* (Ithaca, N.Y.: Cornell Univ. Press, 1978).

33. Mary Kelley, "The Sentimentalists: Promise and Betrayal in the Home," *Signs* 4 (Spring 1979): 434–46.

34. Joanna Russ, "Somebody's Trying to Kill Me and I Think It's My Husband: The Modern Gothic," *Journal of Popular Culture* (Spring 1973), 671.

35. Ibid., 678.

36. Janice Radway, "The Utopian Impulse in Popular Literature: Gothic Romances and 'Feminist' Protest," *American Quarterly* (Summer 1981), 159.

37. Ibid., 153.

38. Carol Thurston and Barbara Doscher, "Supermarket Erotica: 'Bodice-busters' Put Romantic Myths to Bed," *The Progressive* (April 1982): 49.

39. Tania Modleski, *Loving With a Vengeance: Mass-Produced Fantasies for Women* (Hamden, Conn.: Archon, 1982).

40. Radway, "The Utopian Impulse," 148.

41. Ann Douglas, "Soft-Porn Culture," *New Republic* 183 (30 August 1980), 27.

42. Martha Nelson, "Sweet Bondage: You and Your Romance Habit," *Ms.* (February 1983), 97.

43. "Cartland Comes Down Hard on Soft Porn," *Publishers Weekly* (29 April 1983), 28.

44. Thurston and Doscher, "Supermarket Erotica," 51.

45. Helen Hazen, *Endless Rapture: Rape, Romance, and the Female Imagination* (New York: Scribner's, 1983).

46. Joanna Russ, "What Can a Heroine Do? or Why Women Can't Write," in *Images of Women in Fiction: Feminist Perspectives*, ed. Susan Koppelman Cornillon (Bowling Green, Ohio: Bowling Green Univ. Popular Press, 1972), 9.

47. Cawelti, *Adventure, Mystery, and Romance*, 35–36.

2

A Typology of
Romance Formulas

Human kind cannot bear very much reality.

> T.S. Eliot, "Burnt Norton"

Security is having six new Harlequins on the shelf
waiting to be read.[1]

> L.F., Newbury, California

Although the various formulas of romance overlap, as does their
readership, six distinct but related types can be discerned since
midcentury, and all retain some readers today. All romances
focus on love, courtship, and marriage; but thematic concerns
and structural imperatives vary from formula to formula.
Control of sexuality is the central issue of *series* and *erotic* romances, the most popular romance formulas of the 1970s and
early 1980s. The distinctions between them have lessened, although they can still be differentiated, most notably in length
and setting. In the 1960s, the leading formulas were romantic
mysteries that link mystery and love—novels of *romantic suspense* or *gothic romances*—differing from each other in settings and some conventions but sharing a domestic value
structure through which heroines demonstrate competence for
nurturing activities while solving a mystery. Historical novels
delineate a domestic mythology of history in which women's
concerns triumph over social constraints on love, a common
feature of *romantic biographies* about real women in history

and *historical romances* with fictional characters (represented here by the Regency romance subformula).

Series Romances

Series romances provide a baseline against which all other formulas of women's romance can be measured and differentiated, for they are the purest and simplest romance type. Although series differ from each other, they all concentrate on the development of a romantic relationship between two characters. Most issues separating lovers come from within the characters themselves, and external impediments to love play only a minor part. Unlike other romance formulas, series plots are not complicated by extraneous adventures, evil villains, casual sex, external barriers to love, or historical trappings. Readers choose series books in large quantities, seeking out additional experiences of the same type and reading multiple versions of virtually interchangeable stories.

Publishers exert tight control over content and form by limiting length (180 to 250 pages), standardizing cover design, and advertising the series as a unit rather than stressing individual authors. They guide prospective writers by providing an explicit set of rules called a tipsheet.[2] Proliferation of new series, rapidly changing formulas, and increased advertising budgets in the early 1980s reflected the belief of publishers that the potential market remains to be tapped. And the market may continue to grow, for American women read per capita many fewer romances per month than their counterparts abroad.[3]

The original series romances in the United States were published by Harlequin Books of Toronto, an affiliate of the British firm of Mills and Boon; but in the late 1970s, other publishers began to compete for the lucrative and growing market in romances. As series proliferated, distinctions began to emerge. A few (Harlequin Romances, Candlelight Romances) are straightforward love stories; others (Harlequin Presents, Silhouette Romances, Candlelight Ecstasy Romances, and Jove's Second Chance at Love) experiment with more sophisticated situations. Recent series (Silhouette Special Editions, Harlequin SuperRomances and American Romances) feature longer novels and more titillating material.

More than other types, series romances fully exploit the predictability of the marketplace. To be sure, readers recognize other romance novels from external cues on the covers. Gothic romances, for example, include specific features on paperback covers to alert buyers: the woman in the picture wears a diaphanous gown as she flees from a castle or mansion through a hostile landscape. Far above her, a single light shines from the tower. One publishing executive ruefully tells of the time his company decided to omit the light in the turret and found that the innovation failed.[4] Readers of erotic historical romances look for the flowing title, usually three or four words of highly charged language emblazoned across a picture of a man in the act of subduing a passionate and beautiful woman. Some paperback publishers have used the series concept in marketing reprints of especially popular individual authors (for example, Georgette Heyer, Barbara Cartland, and Victoria Holt), but the series romances of Harlequin and its imitators most effectively use uniform packaging to sell a literary product.

Until the number of competing series grew too large for readers to keep up, publishers relied on subscription and catalogue marketing techniques to sell books to devoted readers who apparently did not choose their books by title or author. Unlike mainstream book clubs where members may refuse to buy the current month's offering, romance series services send each month's books to all subscribers. Subscription readers pay the cover price, but they never miss a book and need not inconvenience themselves by making a trip to the bookstore or risk having a particular volume sold out. Some bookstores maintain phone lists of customers to be called when each month's shipment arrives.[5] Consumer research for publishers indicates that romance readers do not recognize the same distinctions among formulas made by publishers and that most romance readers read more than one formula.[6] In 1981 *Publishers Weekly* reported that booksellers stocking a new series of teenage romances published by Scholastic Books discovered that many older women bought these novels aimed at an audience far younger than they.[7]

Harlequin Romances are British imports. When Harlequin began publishing in 1949, it issued Westerns, mysteries, and thrillers; but during the 1950s, romances began to appear more frequently on its lists. In 1957, Harlequin published its first Mills and Boon romance; and after 1964 it published only Mills and Boon books, increasing its annual output of new titles to more than 144 by the late 1970s.[8] Harlequin Presents books appeared in 1973 to highlight the novels of three especially popular and prolific Harlequin writers: Violet Winspear, Anne Hampson, and Anne Mather. Within a year, other Harlequin authors had joined the trio, and new authors who had not written previously for the Romance series appeared in Harlequin Presents, a series that uses the familiar elements of the older formula with a wider latitude on matters of sexuality and a greater sophistication of plot and character.

Harlequin Romances and early Harlequin Presents closely resembled each other. Most books told a simple love story that focused on misunderstandings between lovers and had little overt sexual content. Harlequin Presents, however, changed more rapidly than Harlequin Romances. For example, toward the end of the decade, some Harlequin Presents heroines engaged in premarital sexual intercourse under certain mitigating circumstances; marriage of convenience plots included euphemistic description of sexual relations between the couple; and sexual attraction frequently became the prime motivation.

Later, Harlequin recognized the sexual revolution in its series of SuperRomances, longer books first issued in 1981 to compete with the erotic romances of Kathleen Woodiwiss and Rosemary Rogers. A Harlequin representative described the distinction: "Harlequin Romances take you to the bedroom door; the Presents series open the door; the SuperRomances actually show them doing it."[9] By the early 1980s, however, Harlequin Presents and SuperRomances differed more in length than content.

In 1980, Simon and Schuster's Silhouette series became the

first American romances to challenge Harlequin directly. Simon and Schuster had distributed Harlequin books in the United States; but when the Canadian firm formed its own distribution company, Simon and Schuster began consumer research to determine how best to compete on its own. Silhouette actively recruited Mills and Boon authors, including Anne Hampson and Janet Dailey, who write under the same names for both series, and Charlotte Lamb, who adopted the pseudonym Laura Hardy for Silhouette. Within a year, the American series began distribution in England to compete with Mills and Boon on its home territory. The company invested $5 million in the first year and preceded its initial publication by extensive polling on "everything—from the series' logo to the placement of the gold curlicues on the cover."[10] The company even submitted its proposed advertising campaigns to the panels, and the women chose a promotion featuring Ricardo Montalban of "Fantasy Island" over all the others.[11] Silhouette claimed sales of more than nine million copies in the first six months and projected forty million in the second year.[12] Like Harlequin, Silhouette altered its formula by adding new series instead of making substantial changes in a proven product. In 1981, it announced three new lines aimed at specific romance audiences, two (Special Editions and Desire) with more explicit sexual content and another (First Love) for teenagers. In 1983, it began a series (Intimate Moments) of longer books with wider latitude in plots.

The conscious modeling of the first Silhouette romances on the older Harlequin Presents line started with book design and covers so similar to Harlequin Presents that the Canadian firm filed suit to force a change; and in September 1980, a judge concurred with Harlequin. Simon and Schuster filed a countersuit charging that Harlequin owed commissions earned in previous years.[13] The legal maneuvering indicates the high stakes in the romance market and the nature of Simon and Schuster's gamble.

The early Silhouette romances, like Harlequin Presents, featured virginal heroines substantially younger than the men they married. Despite their more provocative content, however, the novels did not include premarital sex. More recent series romances have a wider range of characters and more explicit sexual content. Some more interesting innovations have come from competing publishers and from more recent Harlequin and Silhouette series. Amii Lorin (Candlelight), Karen van der Zee (Harlequin), LaVyrle Spencer (Second Chance), and Brooke Hastings (Silhouette) write more experimental stories, feature older and more experienced heroines, and explore more "realistic" issues than do some other series authors. Candlelight and Harlequin American Romances have included a few novels with main characters who belong to minority or ethnic groups.

The editor responsible for many series romance innovations, including ethnic characters, is Vivian Stephens, who left Dell for Harlequin in 1981 to edit a new series with North American settings.[14] Her most important innovation for Dell was Candlelight Ecstasy Romances, inaugurated in 1980. The first few titles in this line surpassed the limits of the other series, especially in the depiction of irregular sexual relationships. Heroines in early Ecstasy Romances included unwed mothers, a woman who was sexually awakened at the age of fifteen by her older step-brother, and a thirty-five-year-old doctor in love with a younger man. In Ecstasy Romances, premarital sex became a virtual convention, an innovation that had a rapid impact on other publishers. (Silhouette specifically enjoined premarital sex in its original author's tipsheet, but by early 1981 it published a few books with carefully controlled premarital encounters. In the first, Heather Hill's *Green Paradise*, the editors included a tear-out questionnaire asking for readers' reactions.)

Jove's Second Chance at Love series began in 1981 and included a Regency romance in each month's selections. Heroines have experienced unsatisfactory marriages or love affairs in the past, and they may be reconciled with their previous lovers or husbands or begin once more with a new man. Second Chance also permitted divorced heroines. Its guideline for sexual encounters appeared in the tipsheet for prospective writers:

The hero and heroine make love even when unmarried, and with plenty of sensuous detail. But the explicit details will be used only in foreplay, and the fadeout will occur before actual intercourse. The setting and circumstances of the lovemaking are also crucial and should contribute to the slow build-up of sexual tension. The hero and heroine should not make love too early in the plot. In the Regency novels the sex can stop before intercourse, since the lack of birth control devices creates an element of worry that isn't present in the contemporary romances.[15]

The trend toward "realism" in series romances continued with Ballantine's Love and Life series, whose heroines work out problems within existing marriages or after divorce or widowhood. Avon's series, Finding Mr. Right, requires heroines to choose between two men who offer competing life-styles to the heroine. In 1982, Jove issued a tipsheet for a new series entitled To Have and To Hold: "a couple who is already married when the story opens faces a problem or conflict and resolves it happily, ending with a deeper commitment to each other."

Despite variations, however, all series romances share features that mark them as closely related formula types. They resemble each other in ways that they differ from the other formulas—those that include adventure or require historical settings. Focusing directly on the development of love and commitment between two main characters, series romances are constructed from a group of themes or motifs that may be combined in individual books and that may be handled differently depending on the sophistication of the series.

A series romance begins with a problem or dramatic change in the life of the heroine. She may face a family crisis, begin a new job in an unfamiliar place, or meet the hero, whom she usually detests on sight because he seems arrogant or combative. Characters may actively engage in deception or fall victim to false pride, and an initial white lie complicates matters until the issues become difficult to untangle. Lovers rarely attempt to correct false impressions because they do not wish to appear vulnerable by admitting their love prematurely. Characters go to great lengths to resist their feelings. Some heroines are "spoiled brats" who learn, through the tutelage of the hero, to grow up. When characters meet on the job, the heroine's career ambitions often clash with the hero's. In "desert island" romances, the characters meet in an isolated place, where they gradually learn to love as they cope with their strange situation. In "Latin lover" romances heroines go to an exotic land—the Mediterranean, the Caribbean, the Middle East—notable for hot, passionate men and cultural inequality between the sexes. The hero frequently belongs to the wild environment, and he seems as threatening to the heroine as does the alien landscape. As the heroine responds to him, she becomes reconciled to her role, and he accepts her need for limited autonomy.

Series romances explore the forbidden by providing a fantasy of idealized and controlled sexual expression. Some heroines suffer from past experiences that have made them wary about love. A marriage has failed or a love affair has gone sour. Others have experienced traumatic sexual encounters and have become frozen, unable to respond to normal sexual impulses until liberated by heroes who teach them the distinction between good and bad sex. On occasion, the heroine admits her love sooner than the man, who may have a reputation as a lover of beautiful women. She refuses to become one of his harem, and by holding out for marriage and monogamy she "tames the stud." Many series romance conventions seem anachronistic, especially the "marriage of convenience" plot in which the heroine allows herself to be pressured into marriage with a man she does not love.

Competing series use these motifs differently, especially those with sexual content. In traditional marriage of convenience plots, for example, the pair may defer making love until the ending or later; but in sophisticated novels, the physical relationship in marriage convinces the partners that they love each other—otherwise, of course, they would not be so compatible in bed. When work issues separate hero and heroine, the characters may have difficulty in reconciling their mutual attraction with the demands of professionalism. Career conflicts in traditional series may end with the heroine's capitulation to the hero's expertise, while sophisticated romances feature heroines with serious career commitments who may occasionally win in their controversies with heroes. If the heroine works for the hero, his implied threat has two aspects: he has authority over her professional activities, and his sexual domination controls her personal life. More sophisticated desert island romances exploit the sexual tension between potential lovers thrown together in intimate circumstances. In competing with erotic romances, sophisticated series romances loosened their strictures on portrayals of sexuality. Premarital sex, for example, might be allowed in a novel where lovers had jumped the gun and then faced a long period of separation and reparation for their sins. Some recent romances appear to take female sexual desire for granted.

In all series romances, the shape of the narrative is predictable, even when the outline of a specific plot seems to represent an innovation. Heroine meets hero; problems (mostly of their own making) keep them apart; they come to an understanding and acknowledgment of their mutual love by the last page. Most heroines are in their twenties; few heroes are under thirty, and some may approach forty. Recent series, however, experiment with older heroines and younger, less patriarchal heroes.

Within these predictable patterns, series romances focus with great intensity on that moment in a woman's life when she finds the man with whom she will spend the rest of her life. Among women's romances, series novels represent a "stripped-down" fantasy, focusing on the relationship between the two lovers with virtually all suspense deriving from that one aspect of the story. Usually narrated from the third person point of view of the heroine, the novels consist of a series of encounters between lovers, punctuated by passages in which the heroine thinks about the meaning of what has happened and almost always misinterprets it. Misconceptions fester, but the solution to the problems almost always lies within the power of the lovers themselves. Unlike other romance formulas, extrinsic characters and problems rarely impede the lovers' quest for the perfect mate.

Erotic Romances

Many recent changes in series romances can be attributed to the competition of the other leading contemporary formula, the erotic romance, a story of sexual and exotic adventure or domestic melodrama in a heightened and exciting setting. The protagonists must shift for themselves in a cruel and precarious world, and both external and internal factors separate the lovers. Other characters, including the hero, may victimize the heroine. Erotic historical romances by such popular authors as Rosemary Rogers and Kathleen Woodiwiss include premarital sexual encounters, rapes, or highly suggestive settings (harems, slave plantations). Contemporary erotic novels by Danielle Steel take place in a milieu of affluence, publicity, and sexual corruption. Despite the titillating environment, however, monogamy remains the ideal, even for these heroines.

Not only are individual erotic romances substantially longer than series romances, they sometimes feature the same protagonists in multiple volumes. However, despite the recurrence of characters, erotic romances rarely examine the problems of marriage; instead, they manufacture situations to keep romantic suspense operating despite the heroine's prior commitment to her husband. In Rosemary Rogers's trilogy, *Sweet Savage Love, Dark Fires*, and *Lost Love, Last Love*, the lovers marry two-thirds of the way into the first volume, yet adventures and misunderstandings keep them in a never-ending spiral of rejection and reconciliation, extending through 1,618 pages in paperback.

Erotic romances with contemporary settings may center on issues that seem more modern than preservation of virginity or emotional monogamy. Danielle Steel, for example, treats many subjects not found in even the most sophisticated series romances. One of her heroes serves a prison sentence for rape; some heroines marry much older men before they fall in love illicitly with the heroes. Steel's heroines experience sexual desire, but she is not graphic in descriptions of intercourse. Her women may engage in sex outside marriage but only with men they love. Although they face extreme and dramatic dilemmas, Steel's heroines desire true love and a satisfying marriage while they remain committed to careers. Her heroes recognize the heroines' talents and encourage them to become successful, and she occasionally locates romantic difficulties within existing marriages. She also holds out the promise of redemption from mistakes.

Janet Dailey made her reputation with Harlequin Presents before switching to Silhouette, but she also writes more explicitly titillating romances for Pocket Books. The Doubleday Book Club, a major distributor of romances, offered one of her books with a warning that it contained "explicit sex." Unlike her series books, her erotic romances locate some of the impediments to the lovers outside themselves; and her recent series of erotic romances about the Calder family have settings in the past, common in erotic romances but rare among series books.

Erotic romances represented a significant shift in romance formulas in their rejection of traditional literary and cultural assumptions that had existed for centuries. Until erotic romances allowed heroines to experience sex with multiple partners or find true love despite past sexual mistakes, romance heroines conformed to the double standard of the seduction story. The conventional attitude toward female sexuality was consistent in romances and in other novels with female protagonists that might be called antiromances, books in which heroines who had sexual adventures met a predictable fate.

In antiromances, the double standard reigns in the entire complex of behaviors that pertain to femininity; their heroines behave—sexually or otherwise—in patterns conventionally allowed only to males. They include such works as Gustave Flaubert's *Madame Bovary*, Leo Tolstoy's *Anna Karenina* and, more recently, Margaret Mitchell's *Gone with the Wind*, Kathleen Winsor's *Forever Amber*, and Marcia Davenport's *The Valley of Decision*. In each, the main character does not act according to accepted principles of female social behavior. Often deliberately, she steps over the limits of respectability. Emma Bovary and Anna Karenina pay for their extramarital yearnings by death. Scarlett O'Hara and Amber pay for unwomanly behavior by losing the great love of their lives: Scarlett because she cannot be tamed by Rhett, and Amber because her sexual adventuring makes her unfit for marriage.

The antiromance protagonist appears in formula romances as a secondary character—the beautiful, tempestuous, passionate, and uncontrolled "other woman." The other woman gives in to sexual (unfeminine) urges—whether she actually yields her virginity or not—because she does not recognize the double standard as authoritative. Unconvinced by patriarchy that she cannot behave like a man, she squanders the only capital she has, her virginity, and becomes unfit for marriage or, perhaps, for living at all. In formula romances, she is a negative model for the virtuous heroine, who sees her as a rival. Inevitably, the heroine defeats her because the other woman cannot convert the hero into a husband. Antiromances, however, while sharing the romance value pattern, are about the other woman and have much more potential for titillation than the more restrained formulas.

The protagonist, like Scarlett O'Hara, may marry for the wrong reasons, trapping herself in a loveless union because she settles for less than true love. She is self-deceived, for she may marry a second-best man because she cannot have what she thinks she wants. Since antiromances share with other romances the assumption that each woman has a soul-mate waiting for her, haste always leads to disaster. The antiromance model follows three basic patterns: the woman traps herself through hasty marriage and unfeminine behavior (Scarlett), the woman yields her virginity before marriage and becomes worthless to her true love (Amber), or the woman yields to temptation when either she or her lover is married (or promised) to another (Mary in *The Valley of Decision*). Misery inevitably results from a mistake, because the woman sets herself beyond the reach of the man she wants or betrays her femininity in the eyes of the world. Antiromance heroines have choices, but they refuse to opt for respectability; or, alternatively, lacking choices they still act in ways they themselves perceive as clearly wrong or inappropriate.[16]

As the antiromance developed from and altered the subject matter of the seduction story, the range of possible plots became wider, substituting for the simple outlines of the seduction plot with its sure retribution the more tolerant tensions of Marcia Davenport's *The Valley of Decision*. Its more conventionally admirable heroine is an Irish-American servant who falls in love with the son of the owner of a Pennsylvania steel mill. Aware of their unequal social status, she refuses to marry him, although she allows him to make love to her. She devotes her life to his family and becomes integral to its well-being, and her long service and faithfulness redeem the sin she committed by submitting to him. The book is a love story, but Mary's illicit love dooms her to years of self-effacement and loneliness. Unlike the fallen women in seduction stories, however, Mary achieves a limited triumph.

Until the 1970s, romances and antiromances followed parallel but distinct patterns; antiromances explored the consequences of uncontrolled female sexuality, while romances asserted the value of virginity and domesticity. However, as the traditional limitations of the double standard eroded, publishers responded to the challenge by offering portrayals of female sexuality that had previously been taboo. The historical erotics of Woodiwiss and Rogers resemble *Forever Amber* in their portrayals of sexual adventuring, but the ending differs because erotic romance protagonists make mistakes and still find true love in contrast to Amber's loss. Contemporary erotics explore the territory of infidelity and extramarital sex but offer mitigation and forgiveness to heroines who previously would have had to suffer or die for their transgressions.

The double standard, with its assumption that women had a weak sex drive, began to erode before the sexual revolution, but changes in female sexual behavior continued to occur in private. In the past fifteen years, however, so-called irregular sexual arrangements became public—including a marked rise in couples living openly together and a corresponding decrease in the average age of first intercourse. The facts of female sexuality were, for the first time, publicly at odds with the standards of women's romances. However, erotic romances did not necessarily appeal only to more sexually experienced women. To the contrary, it seems more likely that these new romance patterns provided an acceptable way for more conventional women to participate in the sexual revolution—as onlookers.

Erotic romances combine the elements of several different types of women's fiction. They employ the women's consciousness of all romances and the intertwining of adventure and love familiar to readers of gothics. They frequently borrow the conventions of historical novels to exploit the presumably tougher code of morality in the past, but they differ from other historical romances because sexuality is central to plot development. These books assert that true love can redeem not just the male but also the female and that a woman who yields her virginity need not suffer forever if she yields it to the man she loves and remains steadfast to him. Women can be forgiven their indiscretions in erotic romances, it would seem, because the corrupting forces are usually external impediments to love rather than intrinsic moral weaknesses.

The novels are, of course, punctuated by sex scenes euphemistically described. A few, in fact, are little more than a succession of sexual encounters, most notably Lolah Burford's *Alyx*. The characters are white slaves ordered to breed children for the plantation; and after numerous episodes in the breeding hut, they fall in love. The book includes episodes of oral sex as well as specific reference to genitals: his penis is called his "sex" or "hard rod." For all its titillation, however, *Alyx* employs the romance convention of the pure and innocent virgin awakened to love, for Alyx does not choose to be raped, and she does not voluntarily transgress the code.

LaVyrle Spencer's *The Fulfillment* represents another updated romance convention. Set in rural Minnesota, the book concerns a woman whose husband cannot have children; when he wants a son, he asks his brother to impregnate his wife. The wife and brother resist his request, but they finally succumb to proximity and their developing affection for each other. The sex scenes use an inflated language that underscores the conventional romance situation in which a woman can only be fulfilled by sex accompanied by true love. The heroine experiences her first orgasm with her brother-in-law. As in many romances, sexual expression reveals character but does not serve as an end in itself.

Erotic romances cover a wide range of situations linked by a permissive attitude toward premarital sex and by a willingness to examine subjects previously excluded from romances, such as rape and infidelity. Like other romance formulas and unlike some antiromances, however, their heroines rarely behave promiscuously. Women who gain pleasure from sex with the hero may be horrified and hurt when other men rape them.

Although they may tease and seduce their lovers, they do not approach other men. Unlike pornography, erotic romances do not portray variety as a sexual goal for women. Although erotic heroines do not preserve their virginity, they nevertheless demonstrate emotional—or serial—monogamy.

As romance series respond to the challenge of erotic romances, the formula may decline or change once again. A few writers (Janet Dailey, LaVyrle Spencer, Fern Michaels) now write both series and erotic romances, and the distinctions have blurred substantially in recent years. It seems likely that the erotic romance, as a response to changing sexual mores and a challenge to existing patterns of romance and antiromance, will eventually serve its purpose. If so, its rapid rise provides one more example of the resilience and flexibility of romance formulas over time.

Gothic Romances

Although erotic romances portray women who have adventures, their episodes have little in common with those types of female adventure, deriving from detective and spy fiction, found in romantic mysteries, the dominant romance formula of the 1960s. Although some conventions of the romantic mystery appear in romances over two centuries, their most recent peak of popularity occurred when Mary Stewart, Victoria Holt, and Phyllis Whitney each published approximately one book per year.

Romantic mystery plots have two parallel strands, and each episode moves closer to the solution of a mystery and the uniting of the lovers. The climax occurs when the defeat of the villain frees the lovers to declare their commitment to each other. The gothic romance, one type of romantic mystery, locates its plot in an enclosed domestic setting, frequently an old mansion with an extended family in residence. The source of danger lies within a small group of tightly linked characters. The novel of romantic suspense, on the other hand, has a more open setting in which the heroine may encounter danger from criminals or spies. Prototypical authors of gothic romances include Eleanor Burford Hibbert (writing as Victoria

Holt) and Phyllis Whitney. Mary Stewart set the standard for the novel of romantic suspense.

Literary antecedents for romantic mysteries include authors such as Ann Radcliffe, Mrs. E.D.E.N. Southworth, Mary Roberts Rinehart, and Mignon G. Eberhart. Most important to the modern formula, however, are Charlotte Brontë's *Jane Eyre* and Daphne du Maurier's *Rebecca*. Brontë's Jane and the nameless heroine of *Rebecca* are orphans who must make their own way in the world against great odds. Jane's adoptive family treats her with cruelty, and other characters abuse her. Like other unmarried gentlewomen in nineteenth-century England, Jane becomes a governess, for women of the middle class had few choices. They could become family charges, caring for others but never having a home of their own. They could be schoolmistresses. Or, like Jane Eyre, they could become governesses, existing between upstairs and downstairs, too insignificant for the family's table but too genteel to eat in the kitchen.

Jane Eyre's experience parallels that of innumerable heroines in modern gothic romances. She goes to an old house as a semiservant; she falls in love with a member of the aristocratic family for whom she works; and she has adventures that remove the barriers to her marriage to the hero. Except for Rochester's perfidy in attempting to commit bigamy, Jane's problems resemble those of modern heroines: she lacks the beauty, family, and status that might attract an appropriate husband. But Jane's loveless childhood does not defeat her. She preserves her virginity for a true marriage, refusing the proposal of a man unworthy of her love and waiting until the death of Bertha Rochester before returning to her lover. She redeems Rochester from an unsatisfying life of debauchery; and she wins, through her steadfast action, everything a proper young woman could want: true love, marriage to a man who can give her both status and security, a family for whom she can perform traditional roles, and a triumph over her social limitations. Although the fictional experience, the value structure, and pattern of action resemble the contemporary gothic formula, Brontë far transcends her imitators, especially in the voice of her narrator. Jane expresses anger and rage, thinks more profoundly and seriously about her situation, and engages the reader more honestly.

The nameless narrator of du Maurier's *Rebecca* exemplifies another option for women: marriage to a man she barely knows. Because she has no protecting family to aid her, the naive heroine works as the paid companion of an unpleasant employer. Although the book concerns the relationship between the narrator and her husband, its most notable contribution to the formula came in its portrayal of Rebecca, the quintessential other woman. The narrator compares herself unfavorably to her predecessor until she discovers that Max had hated his wicked first wife. Learning he murdered Rebecca, she protects him; and the last pages show her living in seclusion with her husband, as Jane and Rochester also retire from the world.

The novel that sparked the gothic revival of the 1960s, *Mistress of Mellyn* by Victoria Holt, resembles both these earlier romances. *Mistress of Mellyn*, like *Jane Eyre*, uses the "governess" plot. Another plot pattern, the "suspicious marriage," differs from the marriage of convenience plot of series and historical formulas because marriages in gothic romances are only rarely loveless or mercenary. Although the heroine, like the nameless narrator of *Rebecca*, may not know why her husband proposed to her, she genuinely loves him. In Victoria Holt's *Bride of Pendorric*, the narrator marries a man she barely knows, and the book uses many traditional gothic conventions: identical twins (two sets) who cannot be told apart, illegitimacy, secret diaries, family crypts and portraits, and mysterious music wafting through the house. Its secretive and enigmatic hero could be the villain until he saves the heroine in the final pages. Phyllis Whitney favors the "return to the home" plot: the heroine has lost her parents and wants to solve the mystery of their past. She goes to her ancestral home to meet her family, and her presence threatens to reveal secrets the family would prefer to forget. Most hidden scandals involve sexual infidelity or other domestic irregularities that undermine the nuclear family unit.

All gothic romances, however, share a consistent value system, moral structure, and narrative focus. The heroine usually narrates her own story as she negotiates the precarious problems of solving the mystery and finding her appropriate mate. Gothic romances share with other formulas their location at the chronological point of courtship in a woman's life, but they tell a story with a more confined, claustrophobic, and domestic context.

Romantic Suspense

The romance formula that most closely resembles male adventure fiction is the novel of romantic suspense, best written by Mary Stewart. These books link a mystery and a love story in a contemporary setting where heroines, who are innocent bystanders in a precarious world, have adventures that lead to romantic fulfillment. Some romantic suspense novels—for example, Evelyn Anthony's—are similar to thrillers; others focus on a woman's problem in an extremely dangerous milieu.

Novels of romantic suspense differ most significantly from gothics in their more open settings, wider range of characters, and use of conventions from mystery, detective, and spy fiction. Stewart, for example, draws explicitly on the spy story when she plunges her innocent heroine into someone else's mystery—the thriller's convention of the innocent victim caught in impersonal forces beyond individual control. Frequently, she ends her books with an extended chase sequence, thrusting her narrator into a terrifying series of adventures in the open countryside as she eludes the villain. But her books differ from most novels of international intrigue because of her female narrators, her use of romance conventions to shape the plots, and her apolitical themes. Stewart never relies on political stereotypes to provide motivation for her villains. Two of her books occur close to the Iron Curtain, but in each the villain is a smuggler who uses the border as a convenient escape from the consequences of his greed rather than as a political refuge. In another novel, the villains are former Nazis, but the war crime they committed before the book opens resulted from greed not ideology.

Helen MacInnes, whose thrillers rarely employ romance conventions, provides an instructive comparison with Stewart. MacInnes's books are political thrillers in which labeling a character a Communist or a Nazi proves his villainy. Mary Stewart's villains never get off so easily. In most of her books, they are not the faceless political monsters of spy fiction but characters known to the heroine. Although they may seem sinister, she does not designate them as villains until the end. MacInnes's characters may fall in love, but love does not motivate the plot, and her lovers may be defeated or killed. Stewart always unites the lovers and tells her stories from a female point of view, usually in the first person. Only in *Thunder on the Right*, the book she describes as her least favorite, did she relate her narrative in third person; and most of the story is told from the heroine's limited angle of vision.[17]

Mary Stewart claims, with justification, that the delineation of character is important to her. Her creations are both interesting as individuals and conventionally admirable in morality. She says she does not like to write about depravity and corruption, and her characters convey the qualities she admires.

[The] heroine has to be the sort of person who interests me. I have to like her. I have to live in her. I do try to put myself in these bodies and minds, and think and act the way they would, but to some extent they are bound to like the things I like—I mean, the important things. They have the same general values.[18]

Her heroines do not seek adventure, but when confronted with villainy they do not hesitate to act. They never walk away from someone else's trouble. In *The Moonspinners*, the heroine insists on helping the hero in his search for his brother despite his plea that she protect herself instead. Unlike a gothic romance, *The Moonspinners* does not have either a family secret or a scandal in its plot. It takes place in an open, alien countryside instead of a claustrophobic domestic circle.

The Moonspinners shares with other romances their location at the point of courtship, but it poses more complex problems for the heroine, who must prove her worth to the hero by demonstrating both feminine qualities and the resourcefulness and courage necessary to defeat the villains. Romantic mysteries, unlike series romances, locate impediments outside the couple in a world that threatens to overwhelm love until thwarted by action. Instead of forcing characters into obsessive concentration on human relationships, these books take them out of that confined world and provide an extension of female values in a more exciting context.

In both romantic mystery formulas—gothic and romantic suspense—the heroine acts decisively to solve a mystery, a present crime or a past puzzle. She may have help from other characters—most notably the hero—but her own actions are integral to the solution. Her prime motivation—unlike that of the hero in suspense fiction—is the formation or preservation of the family unit. Forced by circumstances to discover and neutralize the source of danger, she rarely feels a moral imperative to punish the guilty. She acts only to protect the villain's innocent victims and within the confines of conventional female roles and motivations. By performing well within the context of women's traditional sphere, she surpasses all other women in the novel; and her performance constitutes a kind of "domestic test" through which she proves her worthiness for the anticipated reward: the acquisition of a husband, home, and children of her own.

Through identification with the heroine, the reader experiences a world in which excitement, mystery, danger, and action coexist with domestic values and the social roles that women traditionally perform. Crucial to the domestic context of these novels is the precarious nature of female existence, objectified by the actions of a villain who threatens the stability of the family. Villains may murder, but these books are not about the thwarting of criminals or spies, since the center of consciousness and the shape of the story are so firmly seated in domestic values rather than in larger issues of good and evil. The heroine is not a detective, although she occasionally functions as one, since she works to solve the mystery reluctantly, has no desire to act except to protect herself and others, and may seem to be more a victim than an actor.

In romantic mysteries, the conventional female world and all its implications shift from the mundane experience of everyday life to an exciting, romantic, and extraordinary world where they take on configurations that make them more significant and attractive than real life. Romantic mysteries heighten the value of everyday domestic activities by allowing readers to escape to a world in which women's accepted roles and values contribute to the amelioration of fantastic dangers. The performance of the heroine in solving the mystery is a "fantasy of competence," a proof, however oblique, that the conventional values of women's lives—consideration for others, protectiveness toward the weak (especially children and animals), preservation of virginity, intuitive decision-making, unselfish nurturing of those in distress, loving submission to Mr. Right—do not preclude action and adventure. The reward for action, in which a woman obtains a family—or the promise of one—for the rest of her life, is a "fantasy of significance," demonstrating that those same conventional values of womanhood lead to conventional rewards as a natural consequence of feminine behavior.

Romantic mysteries dominated in an era when changing imperatives for women created widespread confusion about female roles but offered few models for solving the new dilemmas of women. By displacing women's anxiety onto villains who threatened domestic values, romantic mysteries skirted the implications of changing social realities. For their brief period of great popularity, they offered a fantasy that reconciled contemporary tensions with traditional behavior patterns. Gothic romances appear today, but only the work of the most popular authors achieves a wide readership. The original paperback gothics of such publishers as Avon, Pyramid, and Ace—staple romances of the 1960s—have disappeared. Victoria Holt and Phyllis Whitney continue to write one book per year, and their previous works remain in print; but Mary Stewart has published only one romantic suspense novel since 1967. Romantic mysteries failed to respond to the sexual revolution, and the tension between adventure and domesticity on which they relied lacks the relevance to contemporary women's concerns that it had in the aftermath of the "feminine mystique."

Romantic Biographies

Romantic biographies fictionalize the stories of actual women in history. A love story from the past shapes the narrative, and authors choose historical figures whose lives seem particularly suited to the romance fantasy. Many romantic biographies feature the marriages or illicit affairs of royalty. In addition, plots include anachronistic ideas about marriage—for example, voluntary choice of mate—that conflict with conventional historical interpretations. Some novels provide a covert examination of sexual taboo, for they frequently center on irregular sexual experiences of heroines—mistresses of famous men, heiresses forced into marriages of convenience, unfortunate wives of brutal noblemen, or innocent women in sexually corrupted situations. The best writer of romantic biographies is Anya Seton; the most prolific authors are Norah Lofts and Jean Plaidy (another pseudonym of Eleanor Burford Hibbert).

Romantic biographies require substantial historical research, since characters actually lived, and authors often try to tell the "truth" when they can. Some do extensive background research and interpret historical sources with care. More pedestrian writers rehash and rework stale and melodramatic material or distort historical events for purposes of great romance or melodramatic tragedy. Romantic biographies share with other formulas an attitude toward the lives of women in the past and, to some extent, a way of interpreting historical events; but authors of romantic biographies work within confined limits, for they must at least pretend to follow the outlines of an actual woman's life in constructing a plot.

Modern readers recognize the value structure of romantic biographies because it shares with other romances assumptions about love, marriage, women's roles, and domesticity. Certain women's lives seem more appropriate to such fictional treatment than others, and authors tend to gravitate toward the same women and the same periods in their choice of subjects. For women who figure more than once, a reader has her choice of several versions of the same tale. Similar types of women, however, appear from book to book. A heroine—through birth, marriage, or an illicit affair—belongs to a powerful man in history.[19] Her ascribed status derives from conventional assumptions about female power and dependency in the past, and the story focuses on a constricted set of roles familiar to modern readers, the traditional roles for women—wife, mother, and homemaker—of other romance formulas.

As Lillian Robinson says, "Literature belongs to women, history to men."[20] In romantic biographies, authors reshape conventional interpretations of history to bring to the foreground women who, in the work of professional historians, exist on the periphery of events; and the arena for historical action becomes constricted as the narrative outline moves inward. The story may unfold in first or third person, but its narrative center and value structure consistently lie within the domestic sphere. The books interpret history from a restricted perspective, showing how events affected the lives of women allied with men who made history. Even when political or social history is dramatic in itself, domestic values measure the significance of public events, for public issues provide barriers for women in their romantic or domestic lives.

For example, wars have a consistent literary function: they provide a convenient excuse for men (fathers, husbands, brothers, lovers) to be absent from home and unavailable to women. Alternatively, politics may, by separating men from women, disrupt social life. When political turmoil draws male attention away from intimate concerns, female activities—parties, clothing, marriage, family—lack an audience. In novels about women of the Tudor period, rivalries between Henry VIII and other European monarchs become political problems that affect domestic behavior. The Reformation resulted from Henry VIII's grand passion for Anne Boleyn, an interpretation that remains constant in novels about all Tudor women from Catherine of Aragon through Elizabeth I. Few Tudor women seem to have genuine religious convictions because their affiliations with competing religious institutions rest on their domestic circumstances.

In romantic biographies, history occurs as a series of domestic dramas with the women wielding power and influence in traditionally feminine ways. Women who actually shaped historical events rarely appear as heroines. Joan of Arc, for example, is not an appropriate character for romance in the mythological past, for her life does not lend itself to an interpretation that would make the power of love the dominant motivation in her life. Romance heroines are usually those women whose birth, love affair, or marriage placed them in significant relationships with the men—fathers, brothers, lovers, husbands, sons—who influenced history.

But the powerful and flexible domestic mythology can make heroines of some women whose lives might not otherwise seem amenable to romantic fantasy. For example, the outlines of the life of Elizabeth I would apparently exclude her from treatment in romantic biographies, but novelists find material in her life by emphasizing certain details that can be manipulated to fit the mythology. Elizabeth, the daughter of Anne Boleyn, is portrayed in romances as a woman who was tragically aware of the precarious position of women. Mindful of her mother's downfall, she refused to marry because to do so would be to put herself under the control of a man who could dilute her power. Set against the example of her half-sister Mary Tudor, who contracted a political marriage and became vulnerable to her womanly feelings, Elizabeth becomes a tragic figure, for her political power came at the cost of denying herself as a woman. The myth attributes her success as queen to her rejection of love.

Elizabeth may also be contrasted with her cousin Mary Stuart, whose biography coincides with the conventional interpretation of women's romances. Had Mary Stuart been a man, the mythology asserts, she would have been less vulnerable to the machinations of people around her and her own female impulsiveness. Romantic biographies about Mary Stuart either ignore or simplify the standard historical controversies in favor of a more congenial interpretation. They suggest that she lived tragically because her society would not allow her to love as she pleased. Virtually all the events of Mary's life derive from her lineage, her marriages, and her vulnerable status as a woman who could be symbolically manipulated as a figurehead. She could not be responsible for her downfall because her gender caused all her problems.

Authors of romantic biographies have elaborated over hundreds of popular novels a mythology of British history that stretches from the medieval period through the Edwardian age. Some periods appear more frequently than others because their dominant personalities lend themselves to domestic drama; as a body of work, romances constitute a composite version of the lives of famous women in the past. Romances about more recent periods loosen the limits on women's lives, assuming that more modern women gained increasing control over their own fates. An author can more easily, for example, justify a mistress in the medieval or Renaissance period than in the Victorian age, when the limits on mate selection apparently became less rigid than they had been. *Never Call It Loving* by Dorothy Eden, better known as a writer of gothic and historical romances, is a romantic biography about Kitty O'Shea, the mistress of Charles Stewart Parnell. It derives from the same set of appealing assumptions about history that make other mistress novels popular, although Eden has to make the illicit affair acceptable in the Victorian era, a more difficult task than that faced by an author who uses the medieval period. Kitty's perspective shapes the novel, and she justifies her relationship with Parnell because of their love and her husband's corruption and connivance in the affair. However, Kitty pays for her adultery by living in obscurity and poverty after Parnell's death.

The mythological outline of romantic history begins in the medieval period, when women had to find love in a brutal and unpredictable age that treated them as property, and continues through royal rivalries during the Wars of the Roses. The Tudor period provides background for multiple romantic biographies because Tudor women can be so easily molded into the familiar narrative of domestic myth. The central character is Henry VIII, a monarch who has fascinated historians, playwrights, filmmakers, and writers alike for centuries. In romances, he appears as a tyrant with good intentions, because in his search for a male heir he paid lip service to the romantic convention of loving one's wife. The story of his loves and marriages proceeds in a series of alternative romantic outlines with different women at center stage. Catherine of Aragon, for example, can be portrayed either as an innocent victim of Henry's ambitions or as a jealous and selfish woman bent on preserving her own position against Henry's forbearance and twinges of conscience. Anne Boleyn figures either as the other woman who wrecked Catherine's marriage or as the sympathetic victim of Catherine's jealousy and Henry's brutality.[21]

The life of Charles II, whose arranged marriage to Catherine of Braganza apparently did not deter him from numerous romantic liaisons, also lends itself to romantic reinterpretation. The women in his life—Nell Gwynne, Barbara Castlemaine, Louise de Kerouaille, and a long list of others—appear in Jean Plaidy's trilogy about women loved by the "lusty monarch." Jean Plaidy also wrote a series of novels about royal love affairs from George I to Queen Victoria. The Victorian age domesticates the narrative by dramatizing the marriage of Queen Victoria to Prince Albert, beginning with a political alliance and ending as a love story. The mythology of history ends with the story of Edward VII, Victoria's heir, featuring the lives of his many mistresses, including Lily Langtry, whose story was dramatized in a British Broadcasting Company production of recent years.

The various simplified versions of historical events as seen through the prism of women's lives are also the main stories and periods emphasized for tourists in England. Consistently, the characters of romantic biographies appear in guidebooks and pamphlets about important historical sites, no matter what else has happened there. For example, at Kenilworth the connections with John of Gaunt, the hero of Anya Seton's *Katherine*, and Robert Dudley, the suitor of Queen Elizabeth, are emphasized over other events of the castle's long and varied history. At Hampton Court, the focus is on Henry VIII and his two beheaded wives, even though little remains of the Tudor site. Guides at the Tower of London emphasize the Tudor prisoners and victims, especially women. These events as elaborated through a historical mythology clearly interest both the casual tourist and the female reader, for they are the very stuff of domestic melodrama most easily translated into contemporary terms.

Readers, no doubt, respond to this fantasy for many reasons; but surely one element of appeal comes from their insistence that women also played important roles in historical events. At least in romantic biographies, women get to play the game. In history books, they appear as cheerleaders or not at all.

Historical Romances

Many writers of historical romances specialize in a specific historical period, and publishers frequently promote these books by referring to their setting: Regency, Edwardian, Tudor, Stuart, Colonial. The books feature fictional heroines who seem more conventionally virtuous than heroines of romantic biographies. Based on the premise that finding one's true love in the past was complicated by social restrictions on marriage, historical romances celebrate the exquisite triumph of characters who assert modern values in circumstances that work to defeat them. Women in historical romances overcome the odds of humble birth or lack of wealth and beauty or transgressions of the social code of behavior to triumph in modern terms. Occasionally, historical romances include adventures, and some characters solve mysteries; but the love story always dominates the plot.

Sharing with romantic biographies a set of assumptions about women's lives in the past, historical romances use history in even more imaginative ways, for they are not limited by biography. Heroines may be members of titled families, but their social status or lasting passion for an unavailable man cannot excuse illicit behavior. Like heroines of romantic mysteries, they stand out from other women because they are worthy of marrying for love in a world that does not value female autonomy. Historical romances rely, as do romantic biographies, on the existence of a hierarchical, class-structured society, but they do not treat class barriers in as rigid a manner. Instead, they use the details of life in the past as a backdrop for a love story in a highly romantic milieu.

Innumerable writers have employed the conventions of historical romance in many periods of history, and a comprehensive analysis of all types would be both unending and redundant. For the past fifteen years, however, one particular historical romance subformula has been so popular and so pervasive that it represents the approach of all. The Regency romance, set in that most ambivalent period between the relative license of the Stuart and early Georgian eras and the repression and respectability of the Victorian age, was elaborated most fully in the work of Georgette Heyer. Heyer's romances are set between 1775 and 1825, although the Regency period actually lasted from 1810 to 1820. The majority, and the best, of her novels occur from about 1800 to 1816, prompting inevitable—and only partially unfair—comparisons with Jane Austen.[22] The popularity of Heyer and other Regency writers spawned American imitations; and today, almost a decade after Heyer's death, many writers still attempt to reproduce her fictional world and her success.

The Regency period is no more appropriate for romances than many other eras, but Heyer showed exceptional skill in suggesting its fictional possibilities. Regency romances transport readers to England, often London, to a society in which women contract suitable marriages through participation in a structured social ritual—the marriage market represented by the London season. A courtship ritual dominates the action of each book and provides a value system against which characters' behavior can be measured. Some heroines flout convention more than others, but all are in danger of ostracism for inappropriate behavior.

The vocabulary of Regency romances, seen outside the context of the novels, may seem arch and sometimes confusing; but for devotees, the language enhances the illusion of being admitted to a secret and special world. Characters care about social status, and encroaching persons may be fended off with "setdowns," clever verbal insults that depress pretensions. An "accredited Beauty" is the hit of the season; a woman who lacks beauty may be described as "elegant" or as "having countenance." A plain woman is an "antidote." Eligible men may be "Corinthians," who wear impeccable but restrained clothing tailored by Weston, drive their teams of horses "to the inch," and "peel to advantage" in Gentleman Jackson's boxing saloon. Their only flaw is that they become quickly bored with the silliness of women who "set their caps" for them. A proposal of marriage is called "making an offer." A less respectable proposition "gives a woman carte blanche." Ineligible men are vain and silly, often described as "Tulips of the Ton," who dress outrageously in an exaggerated manner and are convinced, against all the evidence, of their own grandeur.

Heroes and heroines stand out from other characters, who are silly at best and stupid at worst. Heyer was particularly adept at creating dialogue for "chuckleheads," or for a character described as "henwitted," or "a beautiful peagoose," or "a slow-top." A character may be "prosy," or boring, given to speeches and the issuing of offensive, unnecessary advice. Protagonists rise above the foolishness of other characters because they see through the sham yet still behave impeccably by their own standards. If they transgress the rules of the courtship ritual, they do so for the best of reasons. Most Regency heroines also pass the domestic test.

Publishers and reviewers frequently identify Regency romances with the work of Jane Austen, a more appropriate analogy for Georgette Heyer than for other Regency writers such as Barbara Cartland, Clare Darcy, Caroline Courtney, or Jane Aiken Hodge. For most Regency authors, the comparison derives more from the chronological setting of the novels than from similarities between Austen's novels and modern Regency romances. Certainly not even Georgette Heyer at her best threatens Austen's reputation, but both Heyer and Austen use similar conventions and employ social satire to construct their plots. For Austen, of course, those materials were the stuff of everyday life. For Heyer, they remain historical conveniences.

Heyer and Austen both write about young women of marriageable age whose conventional attributes put them at a disadvantage in the marriage market. Their mothers are either absent or unfit to ease their way, and they must depend on their own wits. They face a similar set of options: marriage, teaching, service, or spinsterhood. Some of Heyer's stock characters are reminiscent of Austen's creations, and her "prosy" bores are similar to Mr. Collins of *Pride and Prejudice*, although not so finely drawn. Her attractive young rakes resemble Frank Churchill of *Emma* or Mr. Wickham of *Pride and Prejudice*. She uses characters of virtue but little understanding like Mr. Bingley. Her older heroes have the maturity and competence of Mr. Knightley.

Austen sets no novels in the highest social circles of Regency England, for Almack's and the London season mean little to her characters. Her men do not have titles, although they are genteel, respectable, and occasionally rich. Although most of her heroines marry above their social status, Austen cares more for their achievement of a satisfying marriage with a guarantee of financial security than for social climbing. Her provincial settings—the countryside, small villages, Bath, and Lyme Regis—differ from the fashionable world of Regency romances, for when Heyer uses these same settings, she does so with numerous references to the glamorous world of London. Austen does not mention the Prince Regent in her work, while modern Regency writers refer to him as a symbol of the titillating corruption of the age.

Austen rarely describes clothing except when characters' preoccupation with dress demonstrates their debased or frivolous values. Balls and dances occur in her novels as the social setting for people in country villages rather than as the fashionable events of Heyer's marriage market. Austen employs much richer material and offers a more varied cast of characters and a sharper, more realistic vision of human foibles. Set against Austen's satire, Heyer's humor has a slapstick quality instead of Austen's finely honed irony. However, Austen and Heyer both delineate silly, fatuous, and restricted social conditions for their protagonists.

A book that spans the range of conventions used by Austen and Regency writers is Austen's unfinished novel *Sanditon*, completed anonymously a few years ago by "Another Lady." Austen wrote most of the first eleven chapters before she died; and, although the fragment is not superior Austen, a reader can imagine how the elements of this book might have come together had she lived to finish it. However, when "Another Lady" picks up the tale, the book degenerates into stock Regency romance, perhaps a little better than many because of the constraints of extending Austen's unique plot line. But Austen would never have used the abduction scene that finishes this book. Her ineligible man would have transgressed the social code more subtly than the character imagined by the later writer. The sober and serious heroine becomes a caricature, and the manipulative and impetuous hero could never compare with Darcy or Wentworth. The satire, even when it builds on Austen's base, is thin and silly, and the characters lose their depth and moral ambiguity when the modern author picks up the tale. At the end of an Austen novel, characters get what they deserve but without the unambiguous absolutes of Regency romance.

The unknown collaborator remains anonymous, but she is clearly familiar with Regency romance conventions. Based on internal evidence, she is neither Heyer (no humor) nor Cartland (too clever); but she may be another writer such as Jane Aiken Hodge, who has written a popular biography of Jane Austen. As with Charlotte Brontë and the gothic romance, Austen inspired the modern Regency formula even though the modern writers are less subtle and less profound. However, as Lillian Robinson suggests, both Austen and Heyer

are saying that the personal *matters* . . . the import of historical fiction for women is to reinforce the notion that the public world, however much its vicissitudes may influence women's lives, is always at one remove from women. And conversely, women remain at one remove from it. . . . It is not so much that this kind of fiction "tells" or "teaches" women something about their nature, role, and sphere. Rather, it repeats what direct experience and dominant ideology have already succeeded in communicating.[23]

As authors rewrite history with women at the center, they shape the past to conform to the romance fantasy, participating with other romance writers in the construction of a setting where the traditional concerns of women—the factors that distinguish romances from other popular formulas—seem crucial to human life. Virginal or erotic, adventurous or domestic, historical or contemporary—all romances dramatize issues that belong to women in culture. Unlike other popular formulas and much serious fiction, romances center on the problems of love, commitment, domesticity, and nurturing. These are values assigned by culture to female sensibility, and they are frequently neglected or devalued. But romances place these female values at the center of the fantasy. Romances are stories of feminine women who make a difference, an assumption that rarely influences either cultural dialogue or artistic expression. As fiction by, for, and about women, romances provide an alternative fantasy for the powerless and forgotten by reshaping the world through woman's experience and heightening and dramatizing those aspects of culture women are socialized to desire.

Notes

1. Letter from a reader, in Flora Kidd, *Personal Affair* (Toronto: Harlequin Books, 1981), 189.

2. Michiko Kakutani, "New Romance Novels Are Just What Their Readers Ordered," *New York Times* (11 August 1980):C 13.

3. Daisy Maryles, ed., "S & S to Debut Silhouette With $3-Million Ad Campaign," *Publishers Weekly* (11 April 1980): 51.

4. Paul Richard, "Paperbacks: The Super Sell," *Washington Post* (13 August 1976): 3.

5. Marylouise Oates, "The Ever-Changing Faces of Romance," *Washington Post* (5 July 1981): G8.

6. Daisy Maryles, ed., "Fawcett Launches Romance Imprint With Brand Marketing Techniques," *Publishers Weekly* (3 September 1979): 70.

7. "Scholastic, Bantam Launch New Teenage Romances," *Publishers Weekly* (3 April 1981): 46.

8. *Harlequin 30th Anniversary 1979* (Toronto: Harlequin Books, 1979).

9. Lee Fleming, "True Confessions of a Romance Novelist," *Washington Post Magazine* (5 December 1982): 38.

10. Kakutani, "New Romance Novels," C13.

11. Ibid.

12. Advertisement, *Publishers Weekly* (8 May 1981): 116.

13. Wendy Smith, "Judge Rules Silhouette Cover Too Similar to Harlequin's," *Publishers Weekly* (26 September 1980): 44.

14. Oates, "The Ever-Changing Faces of Romance," G1.

15. "Love's Tender Tipsheet," *Publishers Weekly* (16 January 1981): 45.

16. Elizabeth Fox-Genovese, "Scarlett O'Hara: The Southern Lady as New Woman," *American Quarterly* 33 (Fall 1981): 391–411.

17. Roy Newquist, *Counterpoint* (Chicago: Rand-McNally, 1964), 569.

18. Newquist, 570.

19. Lillian Robinson, "On Reading Trash," in *Sex, Class, and Culture* (Bloomington: Indiana Univ. Press, 1978), 200.

20. Ibid., 203.

21. Norah Lofts, *The King's Pleasure* (Greenwich, Conn.: Fawcett Crest, 1969); Jean Plaidy, *The Sixth Wife* (Greenwich, Conn.: Fawcett Crest, 1953); *Murder Most Royal* (London: Pan, 1949).

22. For an extended comparison of Austen and Heyer, see Robinson, "On Reading Trash," 200–22; also, Robinson's essay in the same volume, "Why Marry Mr. Collins?" 178–99.

23. Robinson, "On Reading Trash," 221–22.

3

Woman's Sphere: Past and Present

"God's nails, you little dolt," Philippa cried, "you should be down on your knees thanking the Blessed Virgin and Saint Catherine, instead of mewling and cowering like a frightened rabbit. My God, you'll be *Lady* Katherine with your own manor and serfs, and a husband who seems to dote on you as well!"

"I can't, I can't. I loathe him," Katherine wailed.

"Fiddlefaddle!" snapped Philippa, whose natural envy increased her anger. "You'll get over it. Besides he won't be around to bother you much. He'll soon be off with the Duke to fight in Castile."[1]

Anya Seton, *Katherine*

Like other fictional formulas, romances use characteristic settings in the creation of a fantasy world for their plots. Distinctions among settings for fantasy represent different orderings of reality that shape the reading experience. Classical detective stories take place in a confined, rarefied atmosphere, frequently in the upper classes of British society, a milieu that constricts the cast of suspects to a finite number of persons and that allows an author to focus blame on the one guilty person. Hard-boiled detective stories require a fluid, seedy, urban environment in which the detective, as the guardian of virtue, must find the least unjust solution to a corruption that pervades the fictional world. The Western formula works best in a lawless landscape, just as the tensions

of spy fiction develop as the protagonist confronts the insuperable forces of international politics. Setting is crucial to fictional formulas, for it defines potential patterns of action and
prescribes the value system against which characters may be
categorized and judged.[2]

The social milieu of male formulas encourages a thematic
focus on justice and morality in a hostile, dangerous, and corrupting world. Romances take place in a more confined domestic space. In male formulas, heroes overcome threats to their
honor or work for the triumph of justice and truth; the precarious world of romances endangers domestic values of love,
commitment, and individual happiness. Male protagonists seek
to master the hostile environment while romance heroines try
to carve out a domestic niche for themselves against great odds.
All formulas, however, require characters to be tested in extreme circumstances that seem impossible to overcome, and
only certain settings provide the necessary resonance.

For romances, the fictional world must contain specific and
significant impediments to family formation and romantic love,
but it must also heighten the value of women's roles through
its inherent interest and excitement. Romance writers must
dramatize love stories—the triumph of female values—without relying too heavily on the conventional adventure motifs
of popular fiction such as crime, outlaws and Indians, international intrigue, intricate conspiracies, or violence. But all
romances occur in places remote from their readers in space
or time.

Exotic settings enhance the events of the story so the reader
can identify with them, move vicariously with the plot, and yet
not have to fear that the dangers will threaten her directly.
Romances are, in short, good fantasy, for they create a psychic
distance that allows a reader to experience the suspense of romance in a world far removed from her own. All romance settings, however, function similarly in portraying situations in
which exotic problems may be overcome through true love.
Space and time may work together or separately to objectify
the elements that jeopardize lovers, and when a love story
succeeds despite the threatening environment, it represents a
meaningful triumph for a heroine.

Contemporary romances situate heroines in glamorous and unfamiliar places. Series romances may occur in romantic settings like the hot, passionate countries of the Mediterranean or Caribbean, on cruise ships, or in exciting work places—the movie, television, or fashion industries, journalism, sports, or big business. Erotic romances may be set against a background of exciting events in an earlier time, where adventures happen at the turn of a page, or in the upper-class world of fashion, taste, and style typical of books by Danielle Steel. Novels of romantic suspense rely on exotic backgrounds— Greece, France, and other isolated and beautiful places—that cut off the heroine from institutional or family support. Gothic romances set domestic activities against the stable, hierarchical social structure of established families who live on landed estates. Historical novels use the exoticism of the past to increase women's difficulties in achieving love.

In all these formulas, romances invest female roles with significance by removing them from the mundane and locating them in the extraordinary, in a place where being a woman is both fulfilling and exciting instead of boring, unstable, and repetitive. The reader's vicarious fantasy is dual: "Would it not be exciting if this were really my world?" and "Isn't it wonderful in such a precarious world that a woman can control her own fate and achieve meaningful rewards against great odds?" These simultaneous aspects of the fantasy determine the appropriateness of particular settings.

The Romance of the British Isles

Many romances, especially those with historical settings, are set in Britain. Until recently, most authors of romance formulas—except erotic romances—were British writers, although substantial numbers of American women read romances. Britain and America have a special historical and literary relationship that makes British history accessible to American readers. American settings frequently lack the social hierarchy and historical tradition common in romance formulas. Phyllis Whitney's gothic romances may be set in America, but she adapts her conventions from Britain—old established families with ancestral mansions in isolated places. Anya Seton uses American history in several novels, but only when the environment resembles conditions of the Old World. One-third of *Devil Water* takes place in Colonial Virginia, but Seton chooses the aristocratic Tidewater mansions and the colonial capital of Williamsburg instead of the milieu of the ordinary settler.

The special appeal of Britain has long been congenial to the romantic ideal. In the late nineteenth century, for example, rich Americans bought titles and status for their daughters by marrying them to members of impoverished European aristocratic families—especially the British nobility. American industrialists and businessmen were denied institutional recognition of their achievements by a democratic ideology that proclaimed that each person made his own fortune. Although wealth could be inherited, status and worth could not. Without seeking the ephemeral and vulnerable political power that America offered through the elective system, they could crown their success by purchasing social status in Britain. Taken by their families to Europe, American debutantes were introduced to aristocratic men who married them for the money the women could provide to preserve crumbling estates or replenish family fortunes. These women acted out a vicarious American dream of success unavailable in their own country by marrying to gain what America lacked, hereditary social status and power. This imaginative resonance remains strong even in our own time. Books about Jennie Jerome Churchill, for example, have sold well in the past decade, and the British Broadcasting Company (BCC) dramatization of her life was popular in the United States. Romances by Dorothy Eden and Barbara Cartland have told fictional accounts of this Cinderella tale of an American heiress married by her family into the British aristocracy.

Americans have an apparently insatiable desire for details about the lives of royalty. Newspapers in America have covered the British royal family for decades; and the American press made great capital out of the abdication crisis in the 1930s, long before British papers mentioned the story. Even events which have little relevance for Americans attract interest, especially if they feature the pageantry Americans both lack and dislike in their own political system. Every detail of Queen Elizabeth's coronation was reported in this country, with extensive explanations of the symbolism of the ceremony. More recently, live television covered the investiture of the Prince of Wales in 1969, the wedding of Princess Anne in 1973, and the wedding of Prince Charles in 1981. These events had little direct meaning for American television viewers, but they had wide appeal as ceremonial dramas denied to Americans in their own political life.

In a country like the United States, with no hereditary titles, the nobility of Britain occupies a special place. Royalist pretensions by American politicians are criticized relentlessly by the same Americans who are fascinated by the activities of genuine royalty, no matter how powerless they may be in reality. When President Nixon outfitted the White House guards in Graustarkian uniforms reminiscent of the courts of Europe, he became a figure of fun. Families like the Adamses, Tafts, and Kennedys incur censure if they appear to see themselves as a hereditary dynasty inimical to American myths of political equality. But in 1976, a highlight of the Bicentennial was the symbolic visit of the Queen to America. The fascination, of course, also extends to historical characters. BBC productions on the lives of British nobility have been popular in the United States on public television and in syndication, and these stories share fairy-tale elements with romances. Cinderella, Sleeping Beauty, and Snow White all marry their Prince Charmings, not just ordinary men.

British ceremony and glamour provide an appealing background for a love story because a structured social setting seems conducive to great romance. Vicarious experience allows identification with conditions of life for which the reader need not take responsibility. The imaginative relationship between Britain and America—an affinity of history, culture, language, and literature—provides for Americans a way of enjoying the ceremony and drama of a hereditary aristocracy without having to participate in it. The imaginative resonance of a stable, hierarchical world offers both glamour and certainty without requiring Americans to face the potential inequities and limits of such a society on their own lives.

Romances frequently require a world of caste and class for tensions to develop, but the American ideology asserts that there should be no artificial social barriers to advancement. In a fluid and open society with only covert limits on potential marriage partners, romance heroines do not encounter great odds in their search for a proper mate. Most American women marry men of similar background to their own, and the mythology of democracy sets up few artificial barriers of class or family between lovers. The ideology of equality, however, does not remove all limits on the choice of marriage partner, although its restrictions remain unacknowledged and informal, like other covert limits on women's lives prescribed by socialization instead of institutions. Covert limits, nonetheless, still frustrate because they cannot be objectified. In romances set in aristocratic society or British history, the limits on women's lives—circumstances and choice of marriage partner—become tangible and predictable, for love and marriage in the past did not automatically follow one another. Social class imposes strict limits on choice, especially when one potential lover belongs to an aristocratic family in the habit of making dynastic marriages. The tension derives from the radically small number of potential marriage partners in contrast to the theoretically large pool of appropriate men available to modern women.

The Domestic Mythology of History

Women's historical formulas similarly objectify covert limits on modern readers by positing a mythology of women's lives in the past. Conventionally, women in the past sought marriage because it, alone among their few options, offered them a measure of autonomy and status. In romantic biographies, women may agree to be mistresses without incurring adverse moral judgments in the novels because they have few options: their lower status makes them ineligible wives for the men they love. Royal or aristocratic women also face limited choices because they must frequently marry men chosen by others to bring new wealth to their families or cement political alliances. The question of whom to marry for women in the past, according to romances, was more often answered for women by outside forces than by them and their lovers. In contrast to the modern belief that women should commit themselves voluntarily to their husbands, the domestic mythology of history requires almost insuperable limits on marital happiness. If women are regarded as symbolic property to be manipulated by families and husbands, they can rarely find true love; but when a heroine nevertheless achieves romantic happiness, she demonstrates to the reader the power of love in overcoming necessity. If she does not achieve love in her marriage, her life becomes tragic, because her failure was not her fault.

The historical mythology asserts that women in the past did not control their own fates, for outside imperatives of birth and politics made their circumstances almost intolerable. The imaginative historical setting often locates impediments to love in the power relationships of a patriarchal society that devalues women's emotions and desires. Heroines in historical novels fight against the odds. Although they may not win, they make the struggle; and they are not willing victims. If they achieve marital success, their reward is heightened in value.

The pattern of assumption and belief in women's romantic biographies shifts the focus from the concerns of the professional historian—a view of the past dominated by male values—to the conventional issues of romance, with historical interpretation secondary to the "all-sufficiency of love."[3] In the conventional historical narrative, few women have affected the course of history in active and instrumental ways; but romances make a virtue of necessity by attributing power to women acting in their own domestic sphere, influencing the men in their lives and shaping public events by performing their traditional roles in a context that makes those roles both meaningful and glamorous.

Authors usually follow the known outlines of history while interpreting personality and motive in a way congenial to modern readers. Anya Seton's *Katherine*, an especially durable romantic biography, required years of careful sifting of sources and balancing of historians' interpretations. Its hero-ine, Katherine Swynford, was the mistress and third wife of John of Gaunt, the sister-in-law of Geoffrey Chaucer, and the direct ancestor of the Tudor dynasty. The historical record contains few details of her life and omits entirely information on her actual motivations and emotional commitments. Her historical significance derives from family relationships with men—through her lover's powerful position in fourteenth-cen-tury politics and her sister's marriage to the century's most significant literary figure. Because Katherine also happened to be the direct ancestor of the faction that won the Wars of the Roses almost a century after her death, her life story takes on significance from symbolic issues and reflected sources.

From these biographical fragments, Seton interprets Kath-erine Swynford's life as a late medieval version of a modern love story. The tension and suspense of *Katherine* come from her plight as an obscure woman in a society that valued sta-tus over love. Seton has the advantage of strong evidence that the affair was a genuine love match, for the facts of history—such as they are—show that the liaison endured through time and that John of Gaunt, freed in old age from the obligations of dynastic marriage, chose to regularize his romance by mar-rying his mistress. For the professional historian, however, Katherine is an accidental pawn in a political struggle. Seton portrays her as a neglected and significant character in Brit-ish history whose life can be dramatized within the bounda-ries of romance conventions. Her love affair with the colorful and powerful Duke of Lancaster, her connection with Chau-cer, and the triumph of her descendants all inflate her signif-icance in history and give value to her life.

Seton grafts on the known an interpretation that attributes to the fictional Katherine those female values and motivations congenial to modern readers. All she wants, so the story goes, is a peaceful life with the man she loves, surrounded by their children, working out her woman's destiny. Seton justifies Katherine's sexual liaison by portraying her late marriage as a reward for fidelity, the consequence of her nurturing quali-ties, and a vindication—through her descendants—of the painful choices she made.

Seton describes in her author's notes how she uses her research to construct a modern formula story. In *Katherine* she tried, even in the most insignificant details, to be as accurate as possible. She learned to read Middle English and Middle French; she read the major chronicles and literature of the fourteenth century; and she considered the limits and biases of her sources. Chroniclers were less interested in accuracy than in propounding a political point of view, and they relied on rumor rather than eyewitness reporting. They ignored women, for women played only small roles in public events; and they omitted such modern concerns as personality and motivation, leaving much interpretation by historians to conjecture. Literature, Seton acknowledges, is also a distorted source, for the vision of the artist overrides reality and interprets personality in oblique ways. Seton used John of Gaunt's own registers for the names of all servants and retainers in the book, visited all the major sites where Katherine lived, and read widely in the work of historians to acquaint herself with the cultural milieu she would portray. So careful is she about the specific details of historical background that Katherine Swynford's Lincolnshire estate—otherwise unmarked—can be located today by following the directions in the novel.

However, when she describes how she chose to interpret Katherine's life, she is on shakier ground. She admits that little is known about Katherine as an individual, that she figures only sporadically in the historical record, and that her significance derives from her reflected roles as lover, wife, sister-in-law, and mother (or ancestor). But Seton asserts without equivocation that "Katherine was extremely important to English history," and attempts to demonstrate this contention.[4] Her narrative interprets historical events in which John of Gaunt behaved in a magnanimous way, rather than in an unfeeling (masculine) manner, as due to Katherine's softening feminine influence. She makes an additional claim for Katherine's significance when she suggests, admitting she is "treading on dangerous ground, that Chaucer may have had his beautiful sister-in-law in mind in occasional passages, particularly in the *Troilus and Criseyde*."[5]

Historical interpretation in romantic biographies can also

influence interpretation of Britain's historic sites, especially if an individual novel has achieved wide popularity. If Katherine Swynford had not been the subject of a novel as popular as Seton's, she would probably be ignored by interpreters of historic sites, for her years of illicit love might make her less than respectable. However, in Lincoln Cathedral the sign beside her tomb specifically mentions Seton's book:

The Katherine Swynford Chantry
Katherine (1350–1403), Duchess of Lancaster, third wife of John of Gaunt (son of King Edward III), Duke of Lancaster and King of Castile, from whom the Royal Family is descended. At her feet, her daughter Joan, Countess of Westmoreland, grandmother of Edward IV and Richard III. . . . This was the "Katherine" of Anya Seton's well-known historical book of that name.

As one might expect in an Anglican cathedral, the sign does not identify Katherine as John of Gaunt's mistress; instead, it emphasizes her marriage and her ancestry of the royal line. Apparently, the British prefer to forget or ignore the part of her life that provides the dramatic tension in Seton's novel.

History in romances provides a partisan and limited vision of the past in which advocacy of the heroine's position within a domestic drama overrides other events. Romantic biographers do not try to be balanced and fair, even when they claim to be accurate. Writers create motivations and characterization in a modern mode, limited only by information that may not be ignored in the interests of accuracy. If little is known, so much the better, for an author has more latitude to write advocacy history without fear of contradiction. In *Katherine*, Seton has exceptionally malleable material, for the distance from events and the outlines of Katherine's life lend themselves to the kind of fictional treatment she wishes to employ. In other novels, however, she works with less and still creates her story effectively.

Similarly, authors may blend biography with fictional characters. Roberta Gellis's *Knight's Honor*, a book set in twelfth-century England, relies on romance conventions in its anachronistic character development. Her subject is a fictional romance and marriage between Roger, Earl of Hereford (who actually existed), and Elizabeth of Chester (who probably did not). In her "Author's Note," Gellis says the events she describes appear in the *Gesta Stephani*, a contemporary chronicle, but she could find no sources about the personalities of her main characters. "Under these circumstances," she says, echoing Seton, "the author has considered herself free to invent a suitable wife, character, and family for her hero."[6] She tries to be accurate about the details of daily life—descriptions of homes, military techniques, dress, and social relationships—and she uses the concepts of medieval chivalry and honor to suggest motivations for her characters. But, like other writers of historical romances, she shapes her narrative by subordinating public events—the material of professional historians—to the domestic story of Roger and Elizabeth, a relationship she bases on conjecture. "The author has taken some liberty in marrying Hereford to a daughter of Chester (who may never have existed), but the long and faithful association between those two houses may indeed betoken some close blood ties between them."[7]

Like Seton, Gellis ascribes to her heroine anachronistic attitudes and problems more familiar to contemporary readers than to any of Elizabeth of Chester's contemporaries. Elizabeth is portrayed as an independent woman, much stronger than any of the men in the book except her husband. She has refused countless proposals because she fears losing the position of power she enjoys as the chatelaine of her father's estate. When she marries Roger in a political alliance, she fears their sexual relationship; and although she loves him, she refuses to respond sexually, for she believes that through submission she will become merely a piece of property. Through euphemistically described encounters, she holds back until Roger resolves the sexual impasse by making an unrealistic and anachronistic gesture to recognize her value as a person. Roger needs Elizabeth's troops in his campaign, and he agrees to let her swear fealty to him and become his vassal in return for commanding troops in his cause. Because Roger privately gives her the status of a man in his life, she realizes that he must love her for herself. She can then respond to him—paradoxically—as a woman.

Romances are revisionist dramas that place woman's domestic sphere at the center of history, a pattern that lends to heroines a significance denied to women in conventional interpretations of history and in everyday life. Domesticated history in romances is a subversive force that offers a positive and meaningful place for the socialized expectations of modern women. But the mythology of history in women's romances both magnifies and constricts woman's sphere. Within the boundaries of history—and the more remote the historical setting, the less constricting fact becomes—a woman's story offers excitement, glamour, and significance through magnifying the cruelty and exoticism of earlier times. The dramatic events, however, take place within the confines of woman's sphere, showing heroines who share the values of contemporary women and preserve family relationships in a setting that makes the task difficult at best.

Women readers, however, identify with heroines of historical novels because they share a value system. Heroines in historical romances prove their femininity against objectified limits that seem more rigid than the reader's own, so the books provide a covert reconciliation with the conditions women find limiting in real life. Women in history appear to want just what modern women believe they should want: the ability to choose their own mates (and control their lives in that one all-important matter), the opportunity to bear and raise children who will be a credit to them, and the materials out of which to construct a comfortable home. Such achievements may seem paltry in contemporary American society, for the range of approved activities for women may not be fully satisfying. But when romance writers ascribe contemporary motivations and values to women who lived in much more exciting and precarious times, readers can invest their own lives, through identification, with meaning and value.

Historical fiction for women represents an inversion of traditional historical interpretation by offering a vision of the past in which women and their traditional concerns occupy center stage. Conventional history not only underrepresents women, it also devalues woman's sphere. Through retelling the past from a woman's perspective, romances reshape familiar stories for a female audience. Writers like Anya Seton recaptured the lives of women in the past long before the contemporary women's studies movement attempted to recreate women's experience for historians, but Seton's interpretations resemble the work of recent women historians in her insistence that women's lives had equal value with those of men and that women in the past had a significant role in the shaping of public events.

Authors who write about actual historical women face different problems than those who make up their heroines. Some historical romances have real people in the plots, but they usually play secondary roles. Historical romances portray love stories against a specific historical background, and the novels concentrate on the problems of courtship and marriage in difficult circumstances that are also shaped conventionally by the domestic mythology.

Regency Romances and the Courtship Ritual

Historical romances also derive from the assumptions about women's lives found in romantic biographies, but they focus more directly on the process of courtship because they need not conform to biography. Women associated with powerful men have some protection from public censure if the romantic relationship remains intact. Ordinary women in the past, however, have few resources for support unless they marry. Among historical romances, the problems appear most fully in the Regency subformula, specifically in the ritual that regulates courtship. Jane Austen's ironic opening line in *Pride and Prejudice*—"It is a truth universally acknowledged that a single man in possession of a good fortune must be in want of a wife."—provides the basis of the courtship ritual. Modern Regency writers assume that every young woman wishes to be married to a man of substantial social position and enough wealth to support her, but she must attain her adulthood without succumbing to the temptations of a mercenary alliance or yielding her individuality. In the world of a Regency romance, women have no genuine alternatives to marriage, but the clearly articulated and authoritative rules that govern courtship make the task highly problematic.

Young women of good family go directly from the schoolroom of their girlhoods to the marriage market, exemplified by the annual London season when all the genteel and titled of England flock to the city. During the season, debutantes "come out" and attend parties, mingle with the adult world, and signal their availability for marriage. Romances portray the season as an exhausting and expensive enterprise: eligible young people meet each other under carefully controlled circumstances, and parents spend enormous amounts of money to outfit their daughters properly to catch eligible men.

Basic to a young woman's success during the season is her ability to procure vouchers to Almack's, a social club open only to the most respectable families—in Regency vernacular, the *ton*. Almack's is governed by five aristocratic patronesses, powerful matriarchs who must be convinced of a young woman's family background or innate gentility. Vouchers may be obtained for debutantes by older women in their families or through a meeting between the young woman and a patroness, who frequently decides to admit her to annoy someone else. Besides its petty and arbitrary admissions policy, Almack's is stuffy and boring, for it serves only soft drinks and does not allow waltzing. Its parties end early, and, although men of good family need not run the gauntlet of patronesses, they must adhere to a rigid dress code. Even the great Duke of Wellington was once refused entrance because he was improperly dressed. Hostesses in London take their cues from the patronesses and send invitations for private parties only to debutantes who have achieved entrance to the ton. Vouchers are a ticket into the marriage market, issued by whimsical matriarchs whose decisions can make or break a heroine's chances for future happiness.

Once admitted to Almack's and invited to other parties, the heroine enters the second part of the courtship ritual: attraction of an eligible man. For Regency heroines, this step is no less difficult than the first because they frequently lack the beauty or wealth of other women or because they attract only inappropriate partners. A scandal in a heroine's family may

make potential suitors wary. Heroines may be unsophisti-
cated about town life and prone to making social mistakes or
appearing "fast." They do not care about wealth for its own
sake, but they all recognize its role in courtship, for a poor
woman cannot afford to dress herself appropriately for the
season. Heiresses must be wary of fortune hunters. Heroines
may profess no interest in contracting marriage, preferring the
independent life—if they have money—or they may be unwill-
ing to marry men they do not love, refusing to engage in a fu-
tile search for an acceptable marriage of convenience. Because
they may be older than the average debutante, appropriate
husbands are a scarce commodity.

The third and most important part of the ritual tests the
heroine against rigid social rules of conduct. If she trans-
gresses the social code, or appears to, she will face immediate
and permanent ostracism from society, and no man will marry
her. Since Regency heroines rarely have conventional attractions—money, family credentials, beauty—they experience
these rules as barriers. To attract an appropriate man, they
must do something out of the ordinary to catch his attention,
but if they step out of line, they run the risk of flouting the
social code.

Rigid rules shape proper female behavior. Older sisters must
be married before younger debutantes may be presented.
Chaperones escort unmarried girls to social events and serve
as guides in mate selection. If they have no mothers, heroines
must find an older relative or friend to sponsor them, or they
may not attend parties to meet eligible men. Although it may
be acceptable for a woman living in the provinces to go riding
or walking alone, an unmarried woman may not do so in London's parks. All debutantes must be careful to avoid singling
out one man before an engagement; they must not, for example, stand up to dance with the same man more than twice in
an evening. They must recognize and refuse the attentions of
ineligible suitors. Women in mourning may not participate in
social activities; and in large, extended families, relatives
sometimes die at inconvenient times and postpone the heroine's participation in the season. Debutantes must have "conversation" so they can make small talk in public, but they must

not be forward or pert. They must maintain the good favor of the matriarchs who oversee the season without alienating either the men at whom they "set their caps" or other characters less central to the romance. Most important of all, they must not be compromised by spending time overnight in the company of a man. A woman suspected of such an escapade will find all invitations retracted and will have lost her chance forever. And the ritual has a time limit, for if a woman has her first London season and has not attracted at least one eligible proposal, she begins to worry. After two seasons, panic sets in. After three, she is, in Heyer's phrase, "on the shelf."

Like the domestic mythology of history, the courtship ritual in its three phases—admission to society, attraction of an eligible man, adherence to the social code—functions as an effective barrier to romance. Some Regency heroines participate in the ritual and transcend it; others are denied the season but still contract good marriages. A few defy the ritual and still win, despite the expectations of other characters in the book. Once the reader knows the Regency world, the ritual functions without having to be explained. It is taken for granted that the heroine's goal—although she need not admit it—should be a happy marriage with an aristocratic and wealthy man. It is understood that her task will be difficult. It is obvious that she must find some way of showing her worth since she has few natural advantages. To flout the rules is to court social oblivion, and she has little margin for error.

Regency romances set unconventional characters and situations against an extremely conventional society with unreasonable rules and expectations. Regency heroines walk the thin line that separates scandal from respectability, occasionally skip across it (or appear to), and still reach the goal. The reader can identify with a protagonist who sees the arbitrary and capricious nature of social requirements and follows just enough of the rules, while behaving in accordance with values held by modern readers. These plots maintain suspense in the tension between the sprightly heroines and the rigid social code. Moreover, Regency romances occur in a world where women's expertise has value. The London season and the marriage market are directed by women. Stock scenes include heroines preparing their wardrobes, learning to behave with feminine grace, attending parties and balls, actively nurturing others, and redeeming men from lives of meaningless promiscuity.

The Regency period appears in historical romances from the point of view of genteel society instead of the licentious royal family, the subject of a series of romantic biographies by Jean Plaidy. In Regency romances, the code of the ton contrasts with the corruption of the Prince Regent's set, as if the stiffly correct social world were a reaction against the publicized lapses of the corrupt upper nobility. Although many heroes of Regency romances are respected by the Prince and his friends, especially for athletic prowess and fastidious taste, they do not participate in the most corrupt of the Regent's activities. Heyer's heroes are experienced men of the world, but they are also mature and sensitive. They never confuse lust with love or deal dishonestly with a woman. Barbara Cartland, on the other hand, frequently portrays rakes in need of reform by the innocent heroine.

In historical romances, as in other formulas with historical settings, the drama intensifies as the world narrows; and a fictional backdrop of objectified barriers to happiness substitutes for the more covert precariousness of modern life. In these books, the rules are certain—women must behave properly or be doomed—but in the contemporary world, the rules are less certain and therefore more problematic. Heroines of historical romances do not have to question whether they should yield their virginity; their problem is to avoid being compromised, a significantly different issue. Historical romances provide a more certain world against which to rebel, both for the heroines and for the modern reader who seeks rules while she simultaneously resents them. Heroines of romances want to achieve a lasting romance on twentieth-century terms, whether they do so in 1812 or in 1983; and Regency authors take advantage of the fictional limits of history to play out a very modern drama indeed.

The Contents of Woman's World

Gothic romances with historical settings also define impediments to love within the domestic mythology of history but in a more constricted setting where the activities of woman's sphere can contribute directly to the unfolding of the plot. Women manage the family's life in the home while men operate in the outside world. Women's activities serve to transform the income and status provided by the husband into an appropriate environment for the family unit. Because women perform nurturing functions, they have expertise in easing personal relationships within the family and between family members and outsiders. Women provide physical and psychological care for children and emotional support for their husbands when they return from their tiring experiences in the outside world. Women are experts in aesthetic areas: they know how to dress and decorate a home. They bear responsibility for the visual impression of the family received by the world. Their actions and interests coincide as they busy themselves in cooking, sewing, furnishing, counseling, supporting, decorating, beautifying, soothing, and caring. These are activities, not innate traits; women have plenty to do.

The contents of woman's world—her tasks and interests— remain constant, but the quality of her environment depends on the contribution made by her husband. He brings to the family in prestige and wealth the raw material from which a woman creates a family, but an unsuccessful husband limits his wife's ability to project an attractive impression. In gothic romances, heroines perform the functions necessary to woman's sphere while simultaneously acquiring the objects and statuses that belong to it. Moreover, they earn those tangible rewards and intangible benefits in situations of great danger.

Many gothic romances take place in isolated mansions that constrict the setting to a limited space and a specific set of characters while enhancing the value of women's functions. The old house motif shapes gothic plots by confining action to an isolated setting that cuts the characters off from the institutionalized protection of society. Phyllis Whitney, for example, says that the mansion throws her heroine on the mercy of the people who live there and on her own devices. Whitney avoids "an onstage murder because that brings in the police, and I don't want them cluttering up my scene. I am not writing a detective story."[8] Family and mansion are linked because the secrets of the past involve the family and occurred in the mansion. The restricted cast of characters works as it does in detective novels, for any character—except the heroine—could be either a good or an evil influence, and the suspense revolves around how the heroine learns whom to trust and whom to fear.

Old houses in romances represent an almost lost tradition of social hierarchy and tradition, since they are usually surrounded by lesser houses and lesser families that echo the grandeur of a bygone era. The houses represent the social position of their owners, frequently the preeminent family in the community now living in the shadow of its former glory. Some houses are rotting and need repair. Although they remain the center of society in the district, their prominence lies in tradition instead of power. The owners of the houses expend time and energy to keep them repaired, but they fight a losing battle against the forces of democratization and time, for they must preserve tradition in a world that values it less with the passing years.

The houses also represent a vanishing tradition of family life. The families who inherit these houses are obsessive about them, as obsessive as they are about the value of family ties. The houses often include among their residents the remnants of an extended family, half-crazed older relatives and dependent poor relations. Servants may be as jealous of the prerogatives of the house as are actual members of the family. Questions of inheritance are tainted by illegitimacy, insanity, and ancient grudges. This extended family of relatives and servants stands in contrast to the modern nuclear family in which most readers live.

Mansions represent a standard of wealth, power, and behavior that excludes outsiders. In Holt's *Menfreya in the Morning*, the heroine has been jealous from childhood of the house's owners; and when she marries the heir, she feels unworthy of her new position. Through marriage, she obtains the house as a residence along with membership in the family, but her newly acquired status contrasts so markedly with her loveless childhood that she sees herself as a perpetual outsider, subject to slights and dangers as an interloper.

Mansions inspire jealousy because so many people want to

own them or belong to them. People who live there feel special, and they want to keep outsiders in their place. Additionally, hidden chambers and passages can be used by villains for nefarious purposes. Old houses represent worlds of their own; the owners are absolute rulers in their domains. The past haunts the present, and the houses' isolation and intricate social relations give them symbolic and actual power. Forces they can neither see nor control threaten heroines with death and obliteration in an anachronistic setting.

Even the most apparently sinister mansion, however, can be purified by true love. The threat comes from people who use the mansion for evil purposes, not from intrinsic corruption. When the evil has been exorcised, the heroine deserves the house and its traditions, for mansions are a proper setting for a great romance and a "happily ever after" life. That life promises to be a fulfilling one, offering status at the top of the social hierarchy and significance in the performance of female roles as wife to the owner, mother to the heir, and mistress of the grandeur of the estate.

The convention of the old house also encourages a concern with luxuries and objects of art. A preoccupation with clothing and dress is often associated with proper social behavior in the activities appropriate to mansions. In *Mistress of Mellyn*, for example, Holt uses two balls at Mount Mellyn as set pieces for the developing relationship between Connan and Martha. For the first ball, Martha has no appropriate dress, and she must observe the festivities with her pupil from the solarium. During the ball, Connan dances with her, a scene that also occurs in *The Sound of Music*, which is, among other things, a governess story. Martha comments with embarrassment: "I in my lavender cotton and my turquoise brooch, they in their chiffons and velvets, their emeralds and diamonds."[9] Before the second ball, however, she receives a dress, decorative combs for her hair, and a diamond brooch; and she notes that she may now pass as a guest. Ball gowns and jewelry, however, do not make the woman; they merely allow her to mingle without shame in the company of the rich and powerful. A similar convention governs characters' attitudes toward the mansions' treasures, such as antiques and paintings of great beauty and value that the villain covets. As a woman, the heroine must know and appreciate their value, but she must not become so obsessed by them that she loses sight of the value of human life. Villains prefer luxuries to people; heroines find in the luxuries a heightened setting for domestic life.

In other formulas, the contents of woman's world similarly define woman's sphere, but luxuries and wealth always serve a metaphoric purpose in the novels. Only in historical or exotic settings, it appears, do women find satisfaction in performing domestic tasks.

Fairy Tales and Literary Sources

Romance settings frequently come from specific literary sources with special resonance for romance plot development. All writers are indebted to such familiar literary antecedents as fairy tales, governess stories, and other popular formulas with appeal to broad audiences. Among romance authors, however, Mary Stewart is probably the most self-conscious about her sources. Before she began to write, Stewart was a teacher of literature and she frequently specifies her indebtedness to other writers and stories, most notably in *Nine Coaches Waiting*.

Fairy tales and romances both reward heroines with marriage to Prince Charming, but heroines must earn good fortune through domestic behavior. *Nine Coaches Waiting* contains specifically what other romances suggest implicitly about the fantasy world of childhood, rewritten for grown-ups, with the story of Cinderella offering the closest analogy. In the Cinderella story, the heroine is attractive but unloved; she suffers and must go through an ordeal; she deserves marriage; and she marries a hero of a higher social class with whom she lives happily ever after.

The fairy tale occurs in a world of the imagination where magical things can and do occur. Most romances are too rational to rely on the supernatural to explain events, but they depend heavily on settings and props that imply the magical. Many novels use literary sources without emphasis; but in *Nine Coaches Waiting*, Stewart deliberately and consciously refers

to many antecedents of her book as principal points of reference. Linda resembles Cinderella: she is orphaned, attractive,
and worthy of happiness, although she must make her own
living. Significantly, she chooses nurturing work. She proves
her worth through her services to a child, demonstrating her
domesticity as does Cinderella through her housework. The
man she marries belongs to the landed gentry, and the novel
implies that once the problems separating them have been removed, they will live happily ever after.

Like Cinderella, Linda goes to a formal ball at the chateau.
Since the governess stands somewhere between the family and
the servants, she is pleased to be invited but not because her
inclusion implies she has the status to attend. Instead, she
wants to go because, as she puts it, "For better or worse, I was
head over ears in love with Raoul de Valmy."[10] Naturally, she
has no appropriate dress and no fairy godmother to provide
her with one, so she makes her own. When she leaves the ball,
one of her shoes comes off her foot as she runs up the stairs.
In this book, Linda rides in a series of cars instead of a magic
coach, but, as in Cinderella, after dancing with Prince Charming, Linda loses contact with Raoul for a period of time before
the end of her story.

Nine Coaches Waiting also gains imaginative resonance from
other literary sources. Because the heroine is a governess,
Stewart draws on Brontë. When Linda thinks about her situation, she compares herself to Jane Eyre and connects the
chateau with Thornfield Hall. The book ends with a chase sequence more typical of the thriller than the romance. When
Linda awakens Philippe in preparation for their flight from the
chateau, she uses a technique that she remembers reading
about "somewhere in John Buchan."[11] While fully conscious of
the sources of her plot and while deliberately exploiting those
sources to set the ambiance of the book and give resonance to
her story, Stewart continually disclaims those other tales. Linda
refers to herself as Cinderella ironically, saying that romantic
fairy tales do not happen in real life. In making herself a fancy
dress (instead of a suitable one) for the ball, she undercuts the
Jane Eyre analogue. And in denying Buchan's world while
embracing its possibilities, Stewart dissociates herself from the

fantasy while still gaining the advantage of reader recognition.

Other romances may draw implicitly on Snow White or Sleeping Beauty when heroes rescue heroines from a living death. The association of villainy with perverted femininity, common in romantic mysteries, derives from fairy-tale portrayals of witches and inadequate mothers. Some authors refer to previous romances when they show heroines reading novels by Jane Austen or the Brontës or describe landscapes by reference to other literary works. *Nine Coaches Waiting* may be unusual in the frequency and intensity of its parallels with other literary forms, but it is not alone in using them to provide a particular kind of romantic milieu.

Travelogues of the Imagination

Romances with contemporary settings lack the resonance of history and aristocracy, and their settings frequently seem more mundane than those of other romance formulas. Nevertheless, series and contemporary erotic romances also construct an appropriate environment for romance out of less malleable material. Until American publishers entered the series market, the Harlequin romances of Mills and Boon frequently took place in a modern world with values similar to those of the historical mythology. Few series romances have aristocratic characters, for heroes and heroines are normally in the middle class; but most heroes have high status and frequently belong to wealthy families or own landed estates. Series romances rely less on aristocratic trappings, family status, and secure social rules of behavior, however, than on barriers to love based on misunderstandings and competition from other women.

Instead of historical settings, series romances use exotic places to enhance the excitement of their plots, and heroes appear as the most powerful characters in an exciting environment. If the hero is a businessman, he frequently works in an unusual place—a hotel in the Caribbean or a ranch in the American West. Because he is successful in his profession, his social milieu is exalted and glamorous. He can be a tycoon, a

lawyer, a doctor, or an artist, but he moves in the highest social circles and can offer to a woman entry into a special and
exotic world. Contemporary romances set in the world's vacation grounds provide a vicarious travelogue for women who have
never experienced the excitement of more romantic locations
than their own.

As competition from erotic romances and other series drove
out the simpler series romances, editors and authors began to
experiment with new locations for romance. Although the
travelogue remains important, the places described are more
varied, and the environment is as frequently chosen for its interesting content as for its lush, exotic background. Isolated
settings—the wilderness of Alaska, a vacation cottage, or an
island hideaway—can be appropriate to contemporary romance, especially when the lovers are alone. Alternatively,
women in the fashion industry, acting, music, art, or journalism may lead lives exciting enough to enhance the action of
romance. Contemporary heroines may have careers as interesting as those of the heroes; and recent romances find tension in career conflicts or in other less anachronistic problems: older women in love with younger men, or women
traumatized by the sexual revolution. All settings, however,
allow readers to experience situations uncommon in normal,
everyday life.

Danielle Steel, for example, frequently depicts women with
privileged lives whose problems in love contrast with their good
fortune. Her novels are filled with details of the good life: jewelry, leather goods by Gucci, designer clothes, fine wines, impeccable and tasteful decor. Her characters have professions
with high interest value such as art or writing, and they live
in style in San Francisco or New York. Some are minor celeb-
rities who face exposure through gossip and publicity that
threatens romance. Her women triumph over tragic and melodramatic experiences: widowhood, imprisonment, paralysis,
death of a lover, divorce, handicapped children. Her books seem
to convey a reassuring message: even extremely fortunate
women experience domestic trauma that wealth cannot ameliorate.

In all romance formulas, the contents of woman's sphere

suggest that domestic values and definitions of femininity have changed very little despite alterations in cultural norms. As traditional limits on women's lives are eased, many women face options and choices that seem frightening and debilitating. Romance settings objectify women's problems and provide a heightened fantasy to show that even in the most extreme conditions, woman's sphere can be both significant and triumphant.

Notes

1. Anya Seton, *Katherine* (Greenwich, Conn.: Fawcett Crest, 1954), 56.

2. John G. Cawelti, *Adventure, Mystery, and Romance: Formula Stories as Art and Popular Culture* (Chicago: Univ. of Chicago Press, 1976).

3. Ibid., 42.

4. Seton, "Author's Note," *Katherine*, viii.

5. Ibid., x.

6. Roberta Gellis, "Author's Note," *Knight's Honor* (New York: Curtis Books, 1964), 5.

7. Ibid., 6.

8. Phyllis A. Whitney, "Writing the Gothic Novel," *The Writer* 80 (February 1967): 13.

9. Victoria Holt, *Mistress of Mellyn* (Greenwich, Conn.: Fawcett Crest, 1960), 99.

10. Mary Stewart, *Nine Coaches Waiting* (Greenwich, Conn.: Fawcett Crest, 1958), 107.

11. Ibid., 183.

4

The Domestic Test

A great marriage is not so much finding the right person as *being* the right person. Most of the women I know would like to improve their roles as wife and mother, which are primarily concerned with things they *do*. Their role as a woman is something they *are*, and that gets us down to basics.[1]

Marabel Morgan, *The Total Woman*

"My [husband] was a doctor in San Francisco, and for five years I tried to be a 'normal' wife."

"What does a 'normal' wife do?" . . .

"To tell the truth I was never sure. I just knew that whatever it was, I was never doing it."[2]

Danielle Steel, *Loving*

Romances always have female protagonists, but not all women are heroines; only women who pass a domestic test by conforming to a set of expectations in values and activities may earn the reward of being chosen by Mr. Right. Although its requirements have changed over time, the domestic test has shaped the conventions of romance fiction for more than two centuries. Its several aspects conform to the three traditional and interrelated roles of female socialization: wife, mother, and homemaker. Heroines must pass the test in all three areas, but different formulas treat the patterns in characteristic ways or emphasize one area over others.

Heroes in male fiction also pass an implied test, usually a challenge that poses abstract questions of justice and fairness and defines male integrity against an external standard. Romance heroines, in contrast, express integrity through domestic and womanly behavior, which may require a sacrifice of the self to the needs of others. Heroines rarely encounter significant moral questions; instead, they face problems that have solutions in love and commitment. Heroines make decisions intuitively rather than logically, for the domestic test assesses women's performance in solving problems that yield to intuition, charity, compassion, and caring.

The domestic test frequently guides heroines in solving moral dilemmas that would be resolved differently in fiction for men, where solutions serve the cause of justice. At the end of *The Maltese Falcon*, for example, when Sam Spade turns in Brigid for killing his partner, he gives her a long list of abstract reasons for his so-called betrayal, adding that their mutual love cannot outweigh his more important commitments to justice and loyalty. In du Maurier's *Rebecca*, however, the narrator condones her husband's murder of his first wife (for justifiable reasons) and helps him evade the law. Few romance heroines face such a clear-cut moral choice; but when plots require moral decisions, heroines act from motivations of personal loyalty rather than abstractions.

The domestic test confers status on women who behave in traditional modes. It assesses female attractiveness to men and prescribes proper attitudes toward beauty, wealth, and adornments. It requires heroines to maintain feminine qualities that attract heroes without relying on artifice or design. It guides women as they learn to express their sexual impulses at the right time with the proper mate. It places a premium on nurturing behavior toward children and the weak, and it rewards women with traditionally feminine interests in homemaking. Success comes to women who possess the innate traits of good women—sexual control, modesty, intuition, selflessness, caring—but who use those qualities actively to benefit others.

The Domestic Test and Women's Roles

The functions of the domestic test parallel the socialized values of women in culture. Women who do not perform the traditional female roles exist in at least a partial social vacuum, for the assumption of these roles gives a woman the right (or the imperative) to act out her expectations. If a woman lacks domestic status, she must redefine herself; and before she considers activities in the outside world, she usually expects to come to terms with her femininity. Coming to terms does not mean that all women perform domestic roles, a statistical impossibility in a society with more women than men in the population. It does mean, however, that a woman must work out for herself an accommodation with each role, even if she merely constructs a coherent set of rationalizations for her failure to acquire the functions. If she performs traditional roles, social mythology asserts that she should feel satisfied and fulfilled; and if she does not, she may have to admit her deviance or sublimate her nonconformity before she comes to terms with her roles. If a woman lacks significant others for whom she can care, she must justify her failure, at least to herself if not to others.

Women's expectations begin to conflict early in life. In childhood, women are encouraged to develop both achievement and affiliative motivations; but a large part of their self-esteem continues to come from the opinions of others. "Compared with men, women remain more dependent on the love and appreciation of others to determine their self-worth."[3] Socialized expectations lead directly to women's satisfaction through performance of the traditional service roles. But a conflict may arise for a woman, trained along with men to excel, who finds the modes of achievement blocked in adulthood and must rely on affiliative motives for gratification.

American core culture overtly offers its girls the same social role choices in the competitive status hierarchy as its boys, while covertly expecting them to decline the more challenging instrumental roles in favor of low-status domestic roles for which they are paradoxically both over-qualified and untrained. Here is a case of cultural discontinuity, where preparation for adult participation in society is followed by regression to dependency upon husband and children. Her situation constitutes a double bind in which either alternative leads to frustration: if she accepts at face value the invitation to share all areas of responsibility with men, she does so at the cost of denying herself as a woman. If, on the other hand, she responds to the hidden message, leaving the broader social field for the protection of the home, it is too frequently at the cost of denying herself as a person.[4]

Women who choose to accept the challenge of the world outside while simultaneously maintaining their traditional functions in the family may find performance in both areas problematic, because the superwoman syndrome can lead to unrealistic expectations and programmed failures. The fabric of socialization may be inherently precarious for women, because performing in either area may block the other, and the attempt to perform in both at the same time may prove impossible or stressful.

Rapid social change produces conflict by offering competing definitions of femininity, most notably in the recent resurgence of feminist consciousness. Women have access to a variety of conflicting models for life decisions. The most visible publication of the women's movement, *Ms.*, is sold on the same newsstands as *Good Housekeeping* and *Ladies' Home Journal*. Even nonfeminists must confront the feminist position, for the movement receives wide media attention. And there has been a predictable backlash. Women who espouse traditional roles, like Phyllis Schlafly and Marabel Morgan, appear on talk shows as often as advocates of feminism like Gloria Steinem and Eleanor Smeal. For many women, the mere existence of this highly visible debate might cause them to feel defensive about their own life decisions, perhaps made many years before the debate began.

Women's roles cannot exist in a vacuum, for they depend on significant others to reinforce performance, and these others must be found through marriage. Not all women will find husbands, and the presence of significant others may appear highly unstable. Marriage is threatened by a rising divorce rate; mothering, by its built-in termination point when the children grow up. Thus, the roles themselves, once achieved, may not endure. Mothering and homemaking may be exalted in social myth, but each role packages failure with achievement.

Motherhood may seem especially problematic and frustrating because society's expectations are so high. Child-rearing authorities emphasize the importance of close, companionable care of children, ideally performed by the mother. As Elizabeth Janeway says: "The more the importance of the mother-child relationship is stressed by psychologists, the more the adult member of the pair feels the burden of her responsibility and the potential of guilt of failing to live up to it."[5] Additionally, the decline of the extended family strengthens the influence of "childcare experts," who may denigrate the experience of older women—mothers, aunts, neighbors—as old-fashioned and discourage women from relying on their own common sense in dealing with their children. Authorities disagree, but many imply that the burden of nurturing lies with the mother. It is her achievement if children thrive, but it is her fault if they fail. Because women are encouraged to identify themselves and their achievements through the behavior of their children, putting aside for a period of years other kinds of personal development, a great potential for conflict inheres in the mothering role.

Pauline Bart, in her study of middle-aged women in mental institutions, says: "We have all read numerous case histories in which a child's neurosis or psychosis was attributed to the mother's behavior. . . . This inquiry deals with the reverse situation—how given the traditional female role, the children's actions can result in the mother's neurosis or psychosis."[6]

Bart interviewed women who say they were happiest when their children depended on them, and now they feel like "nothing," as if they had nothing left to focus on after their children grew up and left home. Many of these women have also suffered during menopause the loss of children and husband; and, given the exigencies of their roles and the way they have defined themselves, they have lost any independent concept of self.

The role of housewife, or homemaker as it is often euphemistically called, raises other issues. As Karen Horney described it: "Either housework is overrated and turned into a torture for the family or it tires her excessively just as every task that is done unwillingly becomes a strain."[7] Additionally, the time needed to perform domestic tasks has been significantly shortened because of new laborsaving devices and consumer products. The culturally prescribed roles may not provide enough to do or satisfaction in their performance because the tasks themselves have become so simplified. Betty Friedan in *The Feminine Mystique* amply documents her reformulation of Parkinson's Law, "Housewifery Expands to Fill the Time Available."[8] But the expansion of housework to fill time does not make it more satisfying, even when it may be defended as a full-time job. The attitude of many women, even those who profess to be fulfilled by housework, finds its expression in the pejorative phrase, "I'm just a housewife." Housework is necessary—someone has to perform it—and it is not easy, but as a full-time occupation it may not provide a satisfying and productive life for a woman, who nevertheless may believe that it should. Housework never stays done, and there is something innately unsatisfying about doing work that will have to be done over again. In other words, it doesn't feel productive, and it doesn't feel like achievement. Also, the work may seem fragmented, especially when it includes care of young children. As Philip Slater notes, housewives can rarely concentrate, and the laughing references to the "minor disasters" of the day are "an antidote to the knowledge that nothing ever happens, really."[9]

But rejecting traditional role expectations requires significant effort because a woman may find it difficult to challenge the power of social mythology; instead, she takes the line of least resistance by blaming herself for her dissatisfaction. Internalizing society's sanctions and prescriptions requires less risk than challenging social truth. Each accepted area of female action carries with it a threat of insignificance, however society appears to affirm its value. When a woman has internalized the dictum that she must—to obtain identity and satisfaction—achieve a happy marriage, have successful children, and create a "haven in a heartless world" with grace and style, the acknowledgment that she either cannot or wishes not to do so can be profoundly unsettling.

Because society defines happiness for women in the context of marriage, many married women find it impossible to consider the possibility that they may be unhappy; and the so-

cially unacceptable becomes psychologically unacceptable.[10] In
each of the three primary roles for women, modern culture
virtually guarantees instability and dissatisfaction that may
lead to an inevitable overvaluing of love and marriage in
women's psychological predilections. However, an inability to
acknowledge unhappiness and tension does not make problems disappear; thus, the difference between social mythology
and perceived experience must somehow be balanced or submerged. Many aspects of society reinforce the pressure, but
romances stand directly at the center of the issue, for they
dramatize the acquisition of those roles and statuses common
to women during late adolescence and early adulthood when
many hope to find mates who will define their lives forever.

The domestic test in romances objectifies and reconciles these
conflicts as it defines and categorizes female characters; and
its requirements shape romance plots, for the personal development of a heroine requires that she prepare herself not for
autonomous adulthood but for a lifelong commitment to the
hero. When romance heroines face personal problems, the dilemmas raise issues relevant to their readiness for marriage.
A sexually traumatized heroine, for example, must work
through her fears and inhibitions before the hero can recognize her as worthy of his love. A woman who chooses career
over marriage must learn that she can combine them. Because married women must be good mothers and homemak-
ers, a heroine must demonstrate her aptitude for domestic
tasks. Action in romances makes women's values and activities crucial to plot resolution, reinforcing the significance of
woman's sphere.

Creating Families

The domestic test appears most explicitly in gothic romances because the formula has the most constricted setting
and adventurous action. The heroine of Victoria Holt's *Mistress of Mellyn*, a penniless gentlewoman, works as a governess, caring for Alvean, the troubled, only daughter of the owner
of an estate in Cornwall. Martha has none of the conventional
attributes that would allow her to gain the contents of wom-

an's sphere. She lacks beauty; otherwise, she tells the reader, she would be married. She cannot afford to buy the clothes and jewelry that might compensate for her plainness. She has no children, so she must care for the children of others. She has no home of her own, so she must make a place for herself in someone else's household. However, Martha gains everything she lacks through feminine behavior that leads her to solve a mystery.

Martha may not be beautiful, but Connan TreMellyn falls in love with her, after rejecting two other women who have more conventional attributes than Martha. Martha's clothes suit a governess until she receives gifts (a gown from her sister and a piece of jewelry from Connan) that permit her to attend a ball where she can practice being a lady. Martha has no children of her own, but her handling of two difficult children proves her worthiness for motherhood. Most significantly, Martha does not merely join an existing family; she literally creates a family where there had been none before. Connan, aware that his former wife conceived Alvean during an illicit affair with a neighbor, cannot love the child until Martha shows him how to forgive. As Martha sets about creating a family for herself, she passes the domestic test.

In romantic mystery formulas, the actions of the villain, who threatens to disrupt an actual or potential family circle, complicate the heroine's task. If the villain succeeds, the heroine will lose her opportunity to enjoy the domestic rewards she earns through virtuous behavior; and since the villain threatens domestic values, evil may be portrayed as a perversion of femininity. In *Mistress of Mellyn*, the villain is Celestine Nansellock, a neighbor and family friend, deranged by her obsessive desire to be the mistress of Mount Mellyn, not because she loves Connan but because she covets the house. Before the novel opens, Celestine murdered Connan's first wife. Believing Connan would marry her after a decent interval, Celestine pretends to care for Alvean and tries to make herself indispensable in the household. When Martha becomes engaged to Connan, Celestine attempts to murder her new rival. Her villainy derives from her inability to act as a true woman because she allows one part of woman's sphere, homemaking, to dominate the others. In contrast to Martha, she fails the domestic test.

Although Martha comes to Mount Mellyn with none of the traditional roles and possessions of a successful woman, by the end of the novel she has obtained each in such a heightened context that they take on a value all out of proportion to that of the more mundane world. The wife of a TreMellyn has more status than a Mrs. Smith; the mother of the heir to Mount Mellyn has more important responsibilities than an ordinary mother; the woman who makes a home on a landed estate has a more satisfying job than a mere housewife. Additionally, these rewards seem more significant because winning them has required solving a mystery—an action that would not be asked of most women—and running risks that rarely occur in the real world. The confirmation of Martha's success in the domestic test is certified, however, not because she brings a murderer to justice but when Connan chooses her as his wife.

Beauty Isn't Everything

The activities through which heroines prepare to be chosen by men are often problematic. The attraction of a husband—becoming a wife—may be complicated by romance conventions about female beauty. Scenes frequently show women learning to appear attractive, choosing appropriate clothing, or creating an effective appearance that will appeal to men while not giving them the wrong idea about a woman's virtue. Authors frequently include detailed physical descriptions of major characters; but heroines value beauty and attractive clothing less for themselves than as protective armor, for a woman who knows she looks her best deals more effectively with men than a woman who feels unattractive. If the heroine of a series romance falls in a lake or lands in the mud, she becomes embarrassed only because her T-shirt clings to her body and reveals all to the hero; and she responds from a sense of vulnerability rather than outraged vanity. Few heroines are classic beauties. Romances portray women who spend time and effort on their appearances, trying to maximize advantages and minimize deficiencies while still remaining largely unconscious of their effect on the men they wish to attract. But heroines must not be obsessed by appearance, and they must never consciously enjoy the attention mere beauty can bring.

Three kinds of heroines appear in romances, and each has distinct implications for plot development: heroines may be beautiful, ordinary, or plain. Series romances, erotic romances, romantic biographies, and some historical romances feature naturally beautiful heroines, but these characters attract men without artifice or overtly seductive behavior. Natural beauty may serve as an impediment to true love, for an attractive woman may not know whether a man feels love for her or merely lusts for her beauty. Beautiful women risk contracting marriages for the wrong reasons or becoming so accustomed to men who want them only for their beauty that they fail to recognize the difference when the hero offers his love.

In novels of romantic suspense, gothic romances, and some historical romances, heroines are rarely beautiful but may seem attractive in their own way. Because they feel inferior to other women, they must find men who appreciate their good qualities by going beyond first impressions. A novel that features a woman of only average beauty relies on different aspects of the domestic test than do those with beautiful heroines, for a woman with only modest attractions must do something active to demonstrate that she deserves the hero's love. The attributes she calls on to attract the hero may vary, but those qualities must be articulated to compensate for her ordinary appearance; for example, she may demonstrate in compensation that she is nurturing, brave, and selfless.

In a few romances, usually those with historical settings, heroines may be homely or plain. Unattractive women pass an explicit domestic test to make plausible the heroes' attraction to them. In Georgette Heyer's *A Civil Contract*, the heroine is the daughter of a vulgar but well-meaning businessman, who offers the titled hero money to save his estate if he will marry Jenny and give her increased status as his wife. Heyer describes Jenny as almost hopelessly unattractive; however, since she has intelligence and common sense, she accepts her weaknesses and compensates by being an excellent wife and mother.

She wants to make her husband comfortable, and she does not waste time trying to compete with more fortunate women. She also understands her husband's loss of pride when he accepts money from her father, so she sensitively makes it easier for him to take the needed aid without incurring intolerable emotional obligations. Eventually, her husband sees the benefits of having a wife like Jenny and gives up his infatuation with a more beautiful woman.

Although romance heroes may be initially attracted to or repelled by a woman's appearance, they recognize superficiality and appreciate women with feminine qualities beneath the veneer. Unworthy men are never so perceptive. Beautiful women can learn to protect themselves from wrong choices, while ordinary women become beautiful in the eyes of men who love them. Plain women find that the men they love do not need beauty in a wife. In a culture that values both youth and beauty, romances reassure women that they need not be beautiful to succeed. It does not matter, so women are told, that they may not have inherited perfect features or acquired glamour. Men who make appropriate husbands will recognize worth despite the exterior package.

These patterns work most overtly in historical romances with unusually independent heroines who do not follow society's prescriptions for proper female behavior. In Heyer's *Sylvester, or the Wicked Uncle*, for example, the heroine is slightly older than the average debutante. She has had one London season, but she "didn't take." When the hero's mother asks if Phoebe is beautiful, Sylvester replies:

No. Not a beauty, Mama. When she is animated, I believe you would consider her taking. . . . She blurts out whatever may come into her head; she tumbles from one outrageous escapade into another; she's happier grooming horses and hobnobbing with stable-hands than going to parties; she's impertinent; you daren't catch her eye for fear she should start to giggle; she hasn't any accomplishments; I never saw anyone with less dignity; she's abominable, and damnably hot at hand, frank to a fault, and—a *darling!*"[11]

To love such a woman, whom he describes in terms that seem more appropriate for a much-loved and indulged child, Sylvester must look beneath the surface. Phoebe has none of the conventional qualities that would lead a man like Sylvester to marry her. She has no interest in marriage, and she intends to set up housekeeping with her sympathetic governess and support them both by writing romantic novels. Despite her lack of social graces, however, Phoebe is more intelligent, more modest, and more honest than other women in the book. And she deserves to be a wife, for she demonstrates her femininity through nurturing Sylvester's heir, the son of a silly, vain, and unfit mother.

In novels with unattractive heroines, the mother and home-maker roles are integral to the demonstration of female worth. In series and erotic romances, novels that concentrate more intensely on sexual attraction and control, the nurturing and homemaking aspects of the domestic test play a smaller part. Heroines differ in the degree of natural beauty they possess, but their attitudes remain consistent from book to book. A heroine must be modest about her advantages but not ob-sessed by her shortcomings. She may wish she could be as lovely as one of her rivals, but she does not waste time wor-rying about it. By the end of the book, she will learn to make the most of what she has; and she will appear beautiful in the eyes of her lover, blooming under his appreciation of her more durable virtues.

A heroine usually has some of the advantages she needs to earn a man's love, but she must overcome the missing quali-ties in competition with more fortunate women. Wealth bal-ances lack of beauty; beauty balances an undesirable family background; nurturing balances plainness or social insignifi-cance. No matter how innately attractive or marginally plain the heroine may appear, however, she always has a quality of innocence and naivete that sets her apart from other women. The innocence functions as an analogue to virginity, giving her a vulnerability that leads the hero to desire to protect her. A reader might easily identify with such a heroine, for a woman who succeeds despite her handicaps offers a reassuring and compelling model for fantasy.

Nurturing

The domestic test requires a romance heroine to behave appropriately toward weak and innocent creatures—children, animals, invalids, the elderly—and to understand male vulnerability in emotional relationships. Nurturing appears most explicitly in romances when governesses take over the task of raising children damaged by the callous actions of others or when heroines marry men with motherless children. Heroines may demonstrate nurturing, however, in any context where their own convenience and the needs of others come into conflict.

Because the needs of children always come first, heroines choose to sacrifice their own happiness if they believe it necessary to the well-being of a child. For example, if the heroine of a series romance becomes pregnant by a man she believes does not love her, she may not tell him because she believes the child will be happier without a father than in a loveless home. In Heyer's *Frederica*, the heroine devotes herself to raising her orphaned siblings and gives no thought to her growing love for the hero. In Seton's *Katherine*, when John of Gaunt finally proposes marriage, he tempts Katherine Swynford by offering to legitimize their children, an action that will remove the barrier (bastardy) to their upward mobility. "We're getting old, 'tis true," he says, "but we're still alive—and if you feel nothing for me—if too much has passed since we were together—then think of our children, for them at least it's not too late."[12]

In romances, however, self-sacrifice leads to a dual reward that blurs the distinction between individual success and subordination to others. The heroine passes the domestic test by putting the needs of others above her own, but her action also increases the hero's respect for her femininity. In *Nine Coaches Waiting*, the heroine must protect her innocent charge from a plot to murder him for his inheritance. Although she believes intuitively that her lover (who has a plausible motive for harming the boy) is not implicated in the plot, she does not take the chance of trusting him for fear she will jeopardize the child's welfare if she is wrong. Instead of losing her lover, however, she gains his admiration once he understands her motives.

Stewart sometimes uses teenaged characters who need an especially sensitive protection by heroines, for they are too old to require active care but too young to handle the adult world without understanding guidance and a partial shield from its corrupt realities. In *Airs Above the Ground*, Tim Lacy, a boy of seventeen whose parents have neglected him, discovers the heroine in an apparent sexual encounter with her husband, whose identity she has promised not to reveal.

> In the growing light I could see him clearly. There was nothing in his face that one could put a name to, no curiosity, or embarrassment, or even surprise. His features had been schooled to a most complete indifference. He was going to play it exactly as I could have wished.
>
> I think it was his very lack of expression that decided me. Boys of seventeen ought not to be able to look like that. Whatever Carmel and Graham Lacy had done between them to Timothy, I wasn't going to be responsible for adding another layer to that forcible sophistication.
>
> And nothing would serve but the truth.[13]

By choosing her duty to a child over her promise to her husband, the heroine treats Tim better than do his parents. The childless heroine neither disillusions Tim by forcing him to witness her sexuality, like his father, nor stifles him by treating him as a child, like his mother. Through honesty and respect for Tim's individuality, she passes the domestic test.

Stewart uses animals in similar ways. In *This Rough Magic*, Lucy discovers a dolphin helplessly beached on the sand and, unable to pull him to safety alone, insists that the hero help her save his life. The hero, a forbidding and unfriendly man, apparently dislikes her, and she cordially detests him. After their mutual effort, however, their feelings undergo a sudden and dramatic change when their exhilaration leads to a passionate kiss. Lucy's insistence on saving the dolphin also pays off later. Thrown into the sea and left to drown by the villain, she tries to swim to shore, but her strength gives out and the dolphin, who seems to recognize her plight, carries her the final few feet to safety.

Heroes also may need understanding, protection, and sensitivity. The heroine of Karen van der Zee's *Waiting* is a widow in love with a recent widower. His grief separates them until she teaches him to accept his wife's death through her instinctive understanding of feelings he finds difficult to express openly. Throughout the book, she acts as the authority figure, but her functions are confined to the traditional female sphere. Rachel, the heroine of Carole Mortimer's *Hidden Love*, acts with extraordinary selflessness in her sensitivity to the unreasonable demands of the hero, but she asserts herself properly when challenged by an inappropriate man. When her boyfriend demands she stay with him instead of taking a stranger to the hospital, Rachel sacrifices the relationship by refusing his order. Later, when the hero (who does not love her) demands she marry him, she agrees because she understands his motivation. However, when she becomes pregnant, she refuses to tell him because she does not want him to feel responsible for her; and she acts out of her nurturing instinct for the hero in her willingness to leave him rather than force him to remain married without love.

Even short-tempered heroines must demonstrate compassion. In the Harlequin Presents novel *Man's World* by Charlotte Lamb, the heroine has a hair-trigger temper and consistently intimidates people with her sarcasm. Kate's apparent cruelty to others stems from her previous marriage to a sadist who subdued her brutally through sex. After his death, determined never to be vulnerable again, she uses her volatility as a weapon. And even Kate has kind impulses. She loves her parents and does not want to hurt them, so she does not tell them of her husband's behavior for fear it will upset them. She indulges her younger brother even though she knows he is spoiled. She goes out with a man she does not love because she senses he needs a friend, and she helps him reconcile the misunderstandings that have led to his estrangement from his wife. Although she behaves abrasively and carries a chip on her shoulder, especially with men, Kate deserves love because a brutal man caused her behavior, and the hero has the power to heal her emotional wounds.

Creating a Home

The final aspect of the domestic test is homemaking, a role much more difficult to dramatize in romances than either of the others. Housework or homemaking does not have intrinsic rewards that can be idealized; it is, at base, boring, unfocused, and hard to inflate with interest or value. In romances, women demonstrate aptitude for homemaking in an unrealistic setting or an exotic place—for example, on an estate rather than in an ordinary house. These settings offer an environment of wealth and luxury in which care of a home has symbolic meaning. In some romances, the hero has an art collection or an ancient mansion that needs knowledgeable and sensitive care to be maintained. But the heroine need not perform actual housework because she has servants to dust and clean while she concentrates on the more glamorous activities of properly caring for things of value.

Homemaking can also be invested with significance through the desert island motif of series romances. When lovers meet in a wilderness where the everyday amenities are missing, the production of simple creature comforts becomes difficult, challenging, and interesting. In the Silhouette Romance *Winter's Heart* by Catherine Ladame, the hero, who lives alone in the Maine woods, rescues the heroine from a blizzard. She does not know how to cook, but her willingness to learn demonstrates her womanly attributes. In the Harlequin Presents novel *Thief of Copper Canyon* by Elizabeth Graham, a flood strands the lovers in a primitive cabin in the Canadian woods. When the hero goes to find meat for their dinner, the heroine bakes bread, cleans the cabin, and adds such amenities as a tablecloth to their daily life.

Even in a novel where the heroine does not have to perform homemaking functions, the author may indicate her aptitude—perhaps in a description of the homey apartment she has decorated herself with little money or when she expresses her appreciation for beautiful objects. Danielle Steel, for example, portrays heroines with exquisite taste and enough money to decorate their homes in style. Although the ability to make a home may not be the most prominent feature in the novel or even explicitly acknowledged, romances imply that heroines can meet the requirements after being chosen by the hero.

The "Other Woman"

Romances reinforce conventional female activities by posing heroines who pass the domestic test against the "other woman," a beautiful and passionate character who may be sympathetic but rarely admirable. In romantic mysteries, the "other woman" sometimes plays the role of villain or conspirator. In all formulas, she serves as the heroine's main rival for the hero's love. Passionate women in romances fare badly in comparison with heroines even though they may seem enviable, for their overt sexuality corrupts them. They fail in the competition for the love of the hero because they are less capable of passing the domestic test, and they serve as negative role models who reinforce traditional assumptions of proper female behavior.

Since men are attracted to beauties because of physical appearance, these women rely on a transitory, unstable, and shallow quality instead of developing the more enduring virtues of femininity demonstrated by heroines. Most significantly, passionate women lose because they threaten the family through their failure to control sexuality. Functionally, "other women" act as villains or foils for the heroine's domestic qualities, and in these roles they echo two of their predecessors: Blanche Ingram of *Jane Eyre*, an aristocratic beauty passed over by Rochester when he chooses Jane, and Rebecca, the beautiful and villainous first wife of du Maurier's novel. Both Blanche and Rebecca find it easy to attract men, and both are corrupted by it. Blanche is merely unpleasant and silly, but Rebecca is certainly one of the most diabolical "other women" in popular fiction.

The passionate, beautiful "other woman" always seems vaguely distasteful, although she need not lose the contest decisively. In *Menfreya in the Morning*, the heroine feels inferior to a beautiful governess in her husband's home. The governess is not an objectionable character—certainly no villain—but she reveals herself as vain (she takes small quantities of arsenic to improve her complexion) and mercenary (she seduces a local landowner, becomes pregnant by him, and forces him to marry her). Although the hero may find the beauty initially attractive, she cannot keep his affection. "I suppose their affair was sultry," one heroine learns, "though things don't last forever on that level alone. You came along and spoiled everything for her. She wasn't able to hold him."[14] One beauty describes the problem herself: "He liked me, yes. And I liked him . . . but he always held back; he seemed to be aware of something in me which . . . well, how shall we say it? . . . wasn't quite what a gentleman looks for in his wife—not Roc's kind anyway."[15] That something, of course, is her amoral sexuality, caused directly, it would seem, by her failure to develop other feminine qualities to complement her beauty.

Mary Stewart's "other woman" in *My Brother Michael* demonstrates her vulgarity by explicitly describing her sexual interest in the hero:

"Men . . . are all the same mostly. But there really is something about Simon. I expect even you feel it, don't you? On the whole my lovers bore me, but I want Simon. I genuinely do. . . . And I can tell you just what it is about Simon. It's—." [The heroine breaks in because she does not want to hear the reason, but the woman continues.] "It takes me two seconds to know whether I want a man or not."[16]

Such women, while not actually villains themselves, are corrupted through lack of sexual control. More explicitly, beautiful women sometimes help villains by allowing their sexuality to override their nurturing instincts. After aiding her husband in his attempts to murder his nephew in *Nine Coaches Waiting*, one of these women says:

"I—I'm not wicked, Hippolyte, you know that. I didn't want to hurt Philippe, but . . . well, it was for Leon's sake. I did it for Leon. . . ."

The dreadful singlemindedness she showed was ample explanation of how Leon had persuaded her to help him against what better instincts she must have possessed. She wept on, "It was for Leon's sake! Why shouldn't he get something—just this thing—out of life? Valmy was his! You know it was! Etienne had no right to do this to him, no right at all! That child should never have been born!"[17]

Because passionate women do not let their better instincts prevail, they invariably fail.

The contrast between passionate women and the conventionally domestic heroines occurs in the context of competition between women for the attention of men, a basic condition of romances. Very few romance heroines have close female friends of their own age, although they may find emotional support from women who are older and thus out of the competition. And because women may seem unreliable as friends and frequently act against the heroine's interests and welfare, romances consistently reinforce women's identification with and dependence on men.

Mothers and Daughters

The implied competition between women for the love and attention of men also shapes the relationship between heroines and their mothers. The heroine must make her way in the precarious world of womanhood alone, and if her parents are living, they are either unavailable or unfit. Although fathers may have admirable qualities, many mothers play an integral part in the heroine's dilemma. In romances where the heroine must prove her worth by nurturing a helpless and unloved child, she may have a mother who is, at best, nonnurturing and, frequently, a cause of the heroine's lack of self-confidence. The contrast between the heroine's feminine behavior and her mother's lack of nurturing suggests that heroines are especially worthy of marriage because they pass the domestic test intuitively, without being shown how to do it.

Mothers in romances resemble those in many other novels by women whose heroines lack maternal models of behavior or have mothers incapable of helping them. Mothers may be, like Mrs. Bennet in *Pride and Prejudice*, vain, silly, unperceptive, and socially inept. Additionally, they may be absent or—

in Phyllis Whitney, for example—jealous of their daughters or actively harmful in their behavior. The competition between heroines and these antimaternal figures is an oedipal struggle, forcing the heroine to compete with her mother for the attention of her father (and of other men), much as children project their ambivalence about their mothers onto the wicked stepmothers of fairy tales.[18] Jessica, the heroine of Whitney's *Columbella*, for example, has a (dead) mother who was so beautiful and vain that she actively worked to attract any man who showed an interest in her daughter. Jessica recovers her self-esteem through helping a girl whose mother is similarly uncaring, and she is rewarded by marriage to the girl's father after his wife dies. A hero who has been victimized by an unfit wife, of course, can appreciate the finer qualities of the heroine.

In Whitney's *Listen for the Whisperer*, the daughter's oedipal struggle does not require defeat of her mother. Leigh resents her mother, a famous film actress, and feels acutely inadequate. "The dynamic woman on the screen fascinated me," she says. "Beside her I felt like zero. How could any daughter grow up to equal such a mother? Was that what my father wanted, I wondered—for me to be like her?"[19] Leigh's bitterness at her mother's desertion leads her to vow never to fall in love; and when they finally meet, both women disclaim any interest in a mother-daughter relationship. By the end of the novel, however, the heroine recognizes that, although Laura may not be conventional, she can be admired on her own terms; and Leigh moves beyond resentment and rivalry to a more mature, accepting attitude.

Although Whitney uses this motif more often and more specifically than other romance authors, the convention of the antimaternal mother shapes most romances. It suggests the necessity for the heroine to be free of female authority so she can prove her autonomous ability to act, the classic oedipal attitude toward the mother that results from jealousy of the mother-father bond. The mother competes with the heroine, especially for the father's love, and she must be discounted or eliminated before the heroine can act on her own.

The oedipal pattern that informs the relationship between

mothers and daughters contrasts with the conventional fa-
ther-daughter bond. Most fathers, present or absent, are be-
loved and admired by their daughters. Since most heroines
marry men substantially older and more experienced than they,
heroes frequently play paternal roles that displace the sexual
overtones of the oedipal relationship from father to lover. Covertly, at least, most romance heroines lose their fathers' aid
and protection before the beginning of the book and gain by
its end the love and protection of men who can take care of
them. Many of the qualities the heroine looks for and responds to in the hero might pertain as much to a father as a
lover. Similarly, heroes may be attracted to heroines for qualities appropriate to a mother. Like Martha, the heroine can
mediate between the hero and the domestic circle, supplying
the missing ingredient of a woman's nurturance that makes
the relationship whole; and she succeeds despite her lack of a
nurturing mother, rising above the antimaternal model and
proving her natural superiority. Female rivalry works in romances to suggest that the underdog—the heroine—can compete with all other women and can triumph over them.

New Contexts for Domestic Challenge

Changing social values for women have led, especially in series and erotic romances, to portrayals of heroines with more
contemporary dilemmas. Heroines of more recent romances may
not be required to capitulate completely to the traditional demands of the domestic test. Yet even these women demonstrate feminine qualities that ally them with their predecessors. In *The Game Is Played* by Amii Lorin, the heroine
continues her medical practice after marriage, and she says
she does not want children. The hero does not demand that
she bear him a child, but she eventually decides to do so.

A few romances explore reversed role patterns. The heroine
of Brooke Hastings's *Rough Diamond* inherits a baseball team
and falls in love with the star pitcher. Because she is both his
employer and his lover, he resists the relationship. His masculine pride makes him reluctant to become financially dependent on a rich woman, and he wants to be the team's general

manager after he retires without getting the position through her instead of on his own ability. Carole Halston's *Collision Course* has a rich and privileged heroine who loves a self-made man with a chip on his shoulder. Conscious of his social inferiority, he distrusts the sincerity of her love. These heroines may appear to act more aggressively than those in other books because they must understand the hero's masculine pride and convince him that love transcends abstract issues or external judgments.

But romance formulas respond to changing social imperatives for women without losing their essential domestic value system. Recent heroines may have career commitments that are not jeopardized by marriage. They may be sexually experienced before the book opens, and they may face issues that result from changing female life-styles. They may also be committed feminists who convince the heroes that a strong woman poses no threat to the male's need to be dominant in a relationship. The heroine of Elizabeth Neff Walker's *Paper Tiger* is a feminist columnist who marries her editor, the one man who knows precisely where she stands (because he must approve her daily copy) and does not feel threatened by loving a woman who achieves. In recent romances, an understanding hero may accept the heroine's adult commitments and individuality; and although she need not compromise through submission to the hero's guidance, she remains, like her predecessors, a true woman at heart.

The Risks of Failure

Failure to pass the domestic test implies the loss of self just as passing it implies the achievement of adult identity, but the domestic test in romances obscures and simplifies the genuine dilemmas of women in balancing competing and contradictory demands. Adult female identity may be difficult to achieve because its assumptions and requirements are unstable, especially when traditional role patterns come under stress from new cultural imperatives. When options seem too numerous, individual decisions become problematic. The domestic test posits an illusion that appears to answer genuine questions while actually evading them.

The paradoxical values in Barbara Cartland's many volumes of fiction and nonfiction suggest why some women might desire an objective model for female identity and behavior—like the pattern for success provided by the domestic test—for Cartland's ideas reflect the competing imperatives of social mythology. In fiction for adults and advice books for teenagers, she deplores premarital sex and advises her readers to retain their virginity until marriage. "Let me give you a golden rule for any girl or woman as regards romance. Play hard to get. It is the most certain method of maintaining and increasing a man's interest. The serious reason is that reticence on your part prevents your being cheap in his eyes and soiled in your own."[20] However, in her works of "history" and "sociology," Cartland idealizes and glamorizes mistresses she describes as "bewitching women," who may be forgiven their sins against the double standard and admired for succeeding through their beauty and wit because, she implies, they have nothing else to use.

Because she admires women who hold men's interest, Cartland blames failing marriages and male impotence on wives who do not take enough care with their appearances or fail to feed their husbands the proper foods to keep them healthy and interested in sex. She recommends vitamins, honey, and tonics to maintain women's beauty and their husbands' potency. Like Marabel Morgan in the popular American advice book *The Total Woman*, Cartland advocates that men be sole masters in their homes and that women defer to them and manipulate them behind the scenes rather than indulge in arguments. She admires historical women who use clothing to attract men, but she deplores current dress styles that reveal so much of a woman's figure that her mystery is lost. In her nonfiction, she describes a male-dominated society in which unmarried love is sinful; but, although she seems to deplore social sanctions as a barrier to free and open expression of love, in her fiction and advice books she is just as prudish as her heroines.

Cartland admits she prefers men to women because men are more interesting and she likes talking to them.[21] Nevertheless, she professes to believe that women are genetically superior to men and that their special qualities fit them for rearing children and making a home. Although she says her greatest achievements were as a wife and mother, she apparently enjoys her role as a public figure while advising other women to stay in their place:

It seems to me absolutely ridiculous that women should cheat in what is particularly their own province. It is almost a kind of sadism which makes them want to degrade their man, to make him suffer in some way simply because he has given them a home, provided them with children and honoured them by giving over what is, in fact, the most valuable thing he possesses—his name.

The battle of the sexes is something which every woman indulges simply because she is trying to assert her independence while at the same time she is dependent on a man's love.[22]

This diatribe follows her observation that many women expect their husbands to help with the dishes.

If Cartland's prescriptions for women reflect the competing and confusing imperatives many women face in their own lives, the outlines of the domestic test in romances make sense. A woman is expected to do the impossible, to take responsibility for the happiness and well-being of her husband and children, to sacrifice her own interests, and to remain attractive. But she must also retain a secure individual identity that guides her in decisions that lie within her sphere. Although the problems of the domestic test may seem insuperable, heroines evade the disorderly perceptions of daily life by adhering to feminine definitions of reality that can be reduced to simple solutions.

Romances create suspense by constantly presenting the heroine with the possibility of failing to achieve her promised adult roles. They imply that loss of the hero's love represents a simultaneous loss of self. The consequences of failure are most specific in romantic mysteries, for these formulas contain the most intense and specific threat to the heroine. Victoria Holt's gothic romances, for example, are classics of female powerlessness and victimization. They take place in confined, frequently claustrophobic settings, and they feature heroines in danger of obliteration. In book after book, the villain's final move against the heroine threatens her with the danger of being immured in a gravelike place or sucked up in quicksand or destroyed by fire. These dangers threaten the heroine with denial of her individuality and existence as she disappears completely and permanently into oblivion. When the hero saves her, he restores her selfhood and rescues her to both life and love.

Heroes in other formulas rescue their lovers from a symbolic death, a sterile existence without love or children or family. When heroines express their willingness to live alone rather than accept an unsatisfying proposal, they always recognize the bleakness of their futures, and even women who do not wish to marry know what they are giving up. The domestic test rewards women who preserve their virginity (or who are not promiscuous) because they acknowledge the need for love and commitment as a control on sexuality. It confers success on women who demonstrate aptitude for female tasks in preparation for their roles in marriage and motherhood. But a true heroine prefers to rely on herself if the only alternative is dependence on an unworthy man. Romances suggest that women must preserve virginity long enough but not too long; they must resist unworthy men but yield to Mr. Right; they must be attractive, nurturing, and selfless without neglecting themselves; and they must not be unfeminine, a designation that lacks a clear definition in romances as in society.

Feminine and unfeminine behavior are not static concepts. As social pressures on women change over time, specific problems and dilemmas evolve and change. Romance heroines reflect obliquely the alterations in women's concerns from the virgin victims of seduction and gothic novels to the sexually experienced (but usually monogamous) career women of Danielle Steel. Janice Radway suggests that the gothic formula of the 1960s gave way to erotic romances in the 1970s because of subtle shifts in social expectations for women—from the certainties of the feminine mystique through an emphasis on individual development to the "freedom" to express sexuality.

The gothic's fantasy resolution represents, finally, an imaginative compromise between slowly developing psychological needs generated by changing social possibilities for women and its readers' still more powerful desire to keep gender relations as they were. . . . [and]

the increased attention to female sexuality which developed as a consequence of feminism and "the sexual revolution" of the sixties made these same readers more conversant with the equally disturbing idea that women might legitimately seek sexual fulfillment.[23]

The domestic test identifies certain female characters as heroines and others as failures, but definitions of failure and success shift with social priorities and cause women to fear they will be inadequate. Romances reassure their audience because different versions of the domestic test speak to different readers and different eras, but the pattern of relationships among characters in all romances supports the patriarchal convention that a woman derives her fullest identity through a man. Through the elaboration of male roles in romances, the domestic test becomes the vehicle through which a heroine becomes an adult, and her triumph must be certified by the hero— the only character with the authority to validate her life. Even in an age of feminism, changing life-styles, and more permissive sexuality, romance heroines continue to perform the domestic test for an audience of one.

Notes

1. Marabel Morgan, *The Total Woman* (Old Tappan, N.J.: Fleming H. Revell, 1973), 38–39.

2. Danielle Steel, *Loving* (New York: Dell, 1980), 379.

3. Judith M. Bardwick, *Psychology of Women: A Study of Bio-Cultural Conflicts* (New York: Harper and Row, 1971), 9.

4. Georgene H. Seward, "Sex Identity and the Social Order," *Journal of Nervous and Mental Disease* 139 (1964), cited in Bardwick, *Psychology of Women*, 153.

5. Elizabeth Janeway, *Man's World, Woman's Place: A Study in Social Mythology* (New York: Dell, 1971), 156.

6. Pauline Bart, "Depression in Middle-Aged Women," in *Woman in Sexist Society: Studies in Power and Powerlessness*, ed. Vivian Gornick and Barbara K. Moran (New York: New American Library, 1972), 164.

7. Karen Horney, "Inhibited Femininity: Psychoanalytical Contributions to the Problem of Frigidity," in *Feminine Psychology*, ed. Harold Kelman (New York: Norton, 1967), 73–74.

8. Betty Friedan, *The Feminine Mystique* (New York: Norton, 1963), 230.

9. Philip Slater, *The Pursuit of Loneliness: American Culture at the Breaking Point* (Boston: Beacon Press, 1970), 68.

10. Jessie Bernard, *Women and the Public Interest: An Essay on Policy and Protest* (Chicago: Aldine, 1971), 171.

11. Georgette Heyer, *Sylvester, or the Wicked Uncle* (New York: Ace, 1957), 272.

12. Anya Seton, *Katherine* (Greenwich, Conn.: Fawcett Crest, 1954), 615.

13. Mary Stewart, *Airs Above the Ground* (Greenwich, Conn.: Fawcett Crest, 1965), 112–13.

14. Phyllis A. Whitney, *Hunter's Green* (Greenwich, Conn.: Fawcett Crest, 1968), 32.

15. Victoria Holt, *Bride of Pendorric* (Greenwich, Conn.: Fawcett Crest, 1963), 236.

16. Mary Stewart, *My Brother Michael* (Greenwich, Conn.: Fawcett Crest, 1959), 146.

17. Mary Stewart, *Nine Coaches Waiting* (Greenwich, Conn.: Fawcett Crest, 1958), 247–48.

18. Bruno Bettelheim, *The Uses of Enchantment: The Meaning and Importance of Fairy Tales* (New York: Alfred A. Knopf, 1976); Sandra M. Gilbert and Susan Gubar, *The Madwoman in the Attic: The Woman Writer and the Nineteenth-Century Literary Imagination* (New Haven: Yale Univ. Press, 1979).

19. Phyllis A. Whitney, *Listen for the Whisperer* (Garden City, N.Y.: Doubleday, 1972), 8.

20. Barbara Cartland, *Sex and the Teenager* (London: Frederick Muller, Ltd., 1964), 77.

21. Mike Wallace, "The Queen of Hearts," interview with Barbara Cartland on *60 Minutes*, CBS-TV (3 April 1977).

22. Barbara Cartland, *I Search for Rainbows* (London: Hutchinson, 1967), 95.

23. Janice Radway, "The Utopian Impulse in Popular Literature: Gothic Romances and 'Feminist' Protest," *American Quarterly* (Summer 1981): 160.

5

Authority, Patriarchy, and Sexuality

"What will you do if I don't behave as you wish me to, Simon?" she asked evenly. "Hit me? Beat me?"

"No, I've got other methods," he replied steadily, watching her face.

"Such as?"

"Push me too hard and you'll find out, honey."[1]

Jayne Castle, *Gentle Pirate*

A heroine's reward for passing the domestic test comes when she is chosen by a hero who can ease her transition from childhood to adulthood, from father to husband. Like the father, the hero is an authority figure who performs multiple functions. He protects the heroine from the consequences of immature behavior and teaches her how to behave in an appropriate manner as his wife. He must be powerful in traditionally masculine qualities, while retaining the sensitivity to recognize her needs. Male authority can be protective, but it implies a potential danger, for a man must initiate a heroine into sexuality and adulthood, a task only accomplished properly by a hero. Even a sexually experienced heroine may have never had a fulfilling sexual relationship, for she has not yet committed herself permanently or emotionally to a man. The hero has more sexual experience than she, but he lacks emotional commitments and frequently learns from her the context for proper sexual expression. Although heroes and heroines have complementary qualities instead of identical traits, both place a value on domesticity and love.

All events in romances revolve around a woman's awakening to sexuality through the experience of courtship and marriage, a moment the fantasy invests with significance out of all proportion to the everyday course of real life. By implication, a woman's previous experience is a prologue; her subsequent life, an anticlimax. During this brief period of early adulthood, a heroine finds not only her life's partner but her life's identity. Although courtship constitutes only a small portion of the chronology of a woman's life, romances rehearse over and over again those same moments, playing them back, repeating them, expanding them, and concluding them satisfactorily. In the process, romances inflate and order courtship as the supreme adventure for women through tense plots that dramatize the achievement for each heroine of a definitive marriage to a hero who appears remote and unattainable.

Although mate selection represents a crucial decision for women, not to be made lightly, our culture offers little guidance to women as they make their choices. Women experience this significant moment alone, for courtship requires lovers to work out a lonely accommodation, unassisted by family or friends, in an indifferent or hostile world and in the context of other women's failures. By providing a set of clues to identify the hero to the reader, often before the heroine recognizes him, and by demonstrating that even the most extreme and outlandish problems may be overcome, romances portray courtship as an exciting, manageable, and fulfilling experience.

In romance fiction, the moment of truth for a woman occurs when she is assigned to an appropriate marriage partner, and life beyond that moment has little explicit or dramatic value in the imaginative world of the formula. If the part of a woman's life that occurs before that moment is prologue and the rest anticlimax, then it seems understandable that women of all ages might read romances to capture or recapture through fantasy that supposedly supreme moment of their lives. Romances refute the cultural evidence of broken marriages and marital discord by asserting that a reader can leave hero and heroine safely in each others' arms, confident that their relationship, now established after such pain, will last forever. The fantasy evades experience in marriage in favor of dramatizing the tensions of mate selection without reference to the more realistic problems of marriage and mate retention. Romances ignore the adult issues of women's lives by obsessively repeating the fairy tale that has for so long informed fiction by and about women in culture.

Identifying Mr. Right

As Ian Watt points out, fiction conventionally portrays women who marry upward.[2] In modern society most husbands are older than their wives; and romance heroes conform to cultural practice, for they are usually more mature and experienced than the women they marry. Heroes possess great skill and status, either at the top of their professions or as members of the landed gentry. They are self-motivated, stable, and exciting; and they have the resources to support a family in comfort. Two basic male character types recur in romances, and these figures derive from characters used by women writers as early as Ann Radcliffe and Jane Austen. Their occurrence and precise definition vary among the formulas, and each type may play either heroic or nonheroic roles that depend on the appropriateness of an individual character for the heroine. In romantic mysteries, for example, hero and villain may be variations on the same type.

The first character type is the passionate, romantic figure with a past, perhaps most familiar in Charlotte Brontë's Mr. Rochester. The second is the more conventional, sensitive, mature and competent husband-lover, deriving from the heroes of Jane Austen. When the first character type, the passionate lover, plays the hero, his past—like that of Mr. Rochester—seems to make him more attractive by conferring on him the mysterious qualities of a man who, through his experience, knows how to initiate the heroine into adulthood. In a villain or "other man," his past may seem more sinister, with overtones of cruelty, violence, or brutality. The second type as hero has great strength and stability and seems particularly solid and trustworthy. His lovemaking may be matter of fact—even understated—but he knows what he wants from the heroine. In a villain, the second type shows an overdeveloped sensitivity. Passionless or effete, he seems weak or more interested in objects than in love. He may see the heroine as a potential possession instead of as a person. The second figure, however, may be both nonheroic and sympathetic in the role of the heroine's friend, an inappropriate marriage partner but neither sinister nor threatening.

The classification of hero, villain, or friend depends on the man's suitability as head of a family unit. Heroes of both types focus their energy and power on constructive activities that illustrate their capacity to protect and provide for their dependents, but they only want to marry women worthy of their love. A villain represses or misdirects his energy into cruelty or greed; male friends are so weak that they seem ineffective and sterile. These two male figures occur throughout romances, with some authors and formulas favoring one over the other. Series romances use both, but passionate men predominate in erotic romances. Historical novels and romantic biographies feature more passionate than competent heroes, but Georgette Heyer relies heavily on the latter. Among writers of romantic suspense, Victoria Holt favors passionate heroes, while Phyllis Whitney and Mary Stewart usually opt for the competent man. Like heroines and other women, these male figures may occur in opposition to one another, with the particular details of the plot determining the type to fill each role.

All romances use these conventional character relationships, but romantic mysteries make them most explicit because of the wide range of characters necessary for their plot development. Romantic mysteries combine love and mystery, domesticity and danger; and these richer plots require more complex roles and patterns. Among romance formulas, only romantic mysteries usually have enough characters to offer several competing persons for the roles of hero and villain; and these include most of the romance novels in which two men compete for the role of hero until the final page.

Mary Stewart's *Nine Coaches Waiting* and *My Brother Michael* illustrate how these two character types function in all the potential male roles. The hero in *Nine Coaches Waiting* is the villain's son, and together they define the passionate character and show how the dichotomy between hero and villain may be delineated. Father and son resemble each other to a remarkable degree, but Stewart defines subtle distinctions that allow them to be opposite in character. The most significant quality of the passionate male figure is his aura of intense energy, brooding power, and dynamic sexuality.

When Linda first sees the villain, who is crippled, she notes his striking appearance and aura of power despite his handicap. Her first meeting with Raoul, the hero, shocks her because he looks so much like his father, although she intuitively likes him better. Significantly, although both men exhibit the arrogance of the dark, passionate male, Leon's injury frustrates his energy, and he expresses himself through sarcasm and appears sinister and unfeeling. Although Stewart is not explicit, Leon's paralysis has apparently left him impotent and caused him to direct his sexual energy into other, and diabolical, channels. Raoul openly expresses anger but only turns it on those who deserve his wrath. Linda instinctively senses Raoul's vulnerability to his father. Both men have suffered, but Raoul's emotional injuries have not perverted him beyond redemption, as has Leon's bitter reaction to his physical injury. Both Raoul and Leon have sexual experience; but Linda's innocence and love domesticate Raoul with little struggle, while Leon cannot be influenced by a woman.

Raoul's vulnerability stems from his loveless childhood, which has crippled his emotions. Linda tells him she loves him, and he challenges her to behave like other women in demanding that he return her commitment. When she declines to ask for an assurance of his love, he is stunned into uncharacteristic confusion. "Linda . . . Linda, listen. . . . This love thing. This is honest. I don't know. . . . There've been other women—you know that. Quite a few. . . . This is different. . . . I'd say that anyway, wouldn't I? But it is. . . . So now you know. I want you. I need you, by God I do. If you call that love—"[3] Linda senses his honesty and pities rather than resents his inability to express love. At the end, she realizes that he is not really the "Prince charming, the handsome sophisticate, the tiger I thought I preferred."[4] Instead, he is "Raoul, who had been a quiet lonely little boy in a house that was 'not a house for children,' an unhappy adolescent brought up in the shadow of a megalomaniac father."[5]

The passionate hero in modern romances, however, is not as complex as his predecessors, Rochester and Heathcliff. Both have an intense energy that sets them off from the relatively sexless St. John Rivers and Edgar Linton. Both characters are also morally ambivalent, compared with the rather bloodless virtue of Rivers and Linton. Rochester may be redeemable— he loves Jane—and an innocent victim of his deranged wife. However, his attempt to deceive Jane into a bigamous marriage is clearly wrong. Heathcliff's depth of passion for Cathy cannot outweigh the evil in his ruthless revenge on all those around him. The passionate hero in contemporary romances rarely contains those ambivalences in one character, for he lacks what one critic of the gothic novel called "the solipsistic struggle within themselves," a characteristic of the original gothic heroes.[6] Leon is simply evil because his injury has caused him to become bitter and vengeful. Even as a cripple, he inspires scant sympathy. Raoul, on the other hand, does not have genuinely evil impulses, for his dark side lies only in his inability to trust in love, a quality that makes him more attractive because he needs Linda.

Other romance formulas also use variations of the passionate man. Barbara Cartland's Regency romances, for example, portray heroes who may seem dissipated and degraded before redemption; but in a hero the signs of dissipation reveal his need for female redemption, while a villain's corruption is secondary to his greed and cruelty. In *A Halo for the Devil*, successive descriptions of the Duke—a villainous rake—and the Marquis—a redeemable one—illustrate the distinction.

The old Duke was thin and tallow-faced, with deep dark lines running from nose to mouth. There was something almost repulsive about his sneering, thin-lipped mouth and the supercilious disdain of his high arched nose.

He had almost a cadaverous look, and his wrinkled skin and blue-veined hands acclaimed his age. His eyes, however, were still bright and shrewd, and they watched with the irrepressible glitter of a compulsive gamester with every turn of the cards.

The Marquis facing him was in actual years not more than twenty-eight, but he looked immeasurably older. He lounged back in his chair with a languid indifference which in itself was somehow insulting. He would have been outstandingly handsome, had it not been for an expression of contemptuous cynicism and the marks of dissipation on his face.

It was difficult to believe that he could smile, or indeed that he could find anything in life of interest. Only those who knew him well would have guessed that beneath his half-closed eyelids he was alert to every move his opponent might make.[7]

The Duke is repulsive; the Marquis, potentially handsome. The Duke is sneering and disdainful; the Marquis, merely cynical. The Duke is a compulsive gamester; the Marquis, alert and in control. The Duke is evil; the Marquis, merely bored.

The romantic male is mysterious, experienced, strong, usually but not always dark, and described in implicitly sexual terms. He is, therefore, so threatening that he must be domesticated to be a genuine hero. If his energies are, instead, frustrated or channeled into evil, he develops into a monstrous villain. The heroine who wins a passionate lover for her husband has it both ways. He has all the excitement and power to fulfill her romantic yearnings, but because he combines sexual potency and vulnerability, he can be domesticated. The heroine gains the sexual and romantic excitement of being loved by such a man and protection through his love from the threat of violation by the outside world—or by him when she submits, sexually or emotionally.

Jane Austen's novels define the second hero figure. Both Darcy in *Pride and Prejudice* and Knightley in *Emma*, for example, are conventional men who raise conventionality to a high degree of virtue. Both have the ability to attract, support, and protect a wife through their competence in the social world. Although they frequently lack the mysterious energy of the passionate figure, they make appropriate husbands through their superiority to all other male characters in the book. Neither Knightley nor Darcy has a past to live down; each manifests his superiority in intelligence, sensitivity, manners, and wit. Knightley has the added advantage of maturity, for he is considerably older than Emma; and through much of the book, he serves as a surrogate father to her rather than a potential lover. These men may not seem to need the heroine's softening influence so much as do the passionate men, although Darcy needs someone to take him down a peg or two and teach him to laugh. They appeal, however, because of their implicit stability, their self-knowledge, and the status they can confer through marriage. If this figure seems more mature and sensitive than other men, and more attractive and intelligent, he offers an assurance of sexual fidelity because he knows his own mind in choosing the heroine. His sensitivity guarantees that he will understand her and consider her needs. He is, in short, a man to be trusted with a woman's identity and her future.

Although not so explicitly sexual as the romantic male, he appears equally authoritative. His strength and power derive from self-assurance, self-control, and uncompromising moral principles, which prepare him to appreciate the heroine. Without strength, he cannot be a proper husband. Without sensitivity, his protectiveness might be unwelcome because it would be too overpowering (as it may be when he fills the "friend" role). The heroine's description of the hero in *My Brother Michael* demonstrates the appeal of this hero type.

> I reflected, as I looked down at him thoughtfully, that it would probably take a good deal to worry Simon Lester. That quiet manner, that air of being casually and good-temperedly on terms with life . . . with it all went something that is particularly hard to describe. To say that he knew what he wanted and took it, would be to give the wrong impression; it was rather that whatever decisions he had to make, were made, and then dismissed—this with an ease that argued an almost frightening brand of self-confidence.
>
> I don't know how much of this I saw in him on that first day; it may be that I simply recognized straightaway the presence of qualities I myself so conspicuously lacked. . . . I only know that I felt obscurely grateful to Simon for not having made me feel too much of a fool, and, less obscurely, for having so calmly undertaken to help me.[8]

Camilla perceives Simon's competence as protective because he also understands her need to not "feel too much of a fool" in contrast to his overwhelming superiority. His combination of sensitivity and protectiveness makes him a man to be trusted, one with whom a woman can reliably ally herself.

Like the passionate man, this second figure may also be cast as an inappropriate husband when he cannot be domesticated. As a villain, he may be obsessed with greed or be half mad. In Stewart's *This Rough Magic*, the villain seems charming, helpful, and generous to those around him, but he attempts murder when a character discovers his sideline as a smuggler. In *Touch Not the Cat*, the villains are the heroine's cousins. Because she thinks of them as brothers, she does not suspect them of trying to harm her. They appear less sinister than the passionate villain, but they nevertheless kill and steal to avoid bankruptcy.

A secondary character in *Nine Coaches Waiting* exemplifies the second male figure in the role of friend. William Blake plays a minor role as Linda's confidant, but he seems too emasculated and soft to be a hero. Although he appears interested in her, he does not protest when she gently indicates she does not want to go out with him. She jokes with him about his name, and she privately identifies him with the poet Blake's little lamb. He comes to her rescue when she calls him, but he offers sympathy instead of help. Blake is kind and benign but less powerful and interesting than Raoul. "Friends" fade into the background in comparison with the more colorful and dynamic heroes, for their lack of the sexual power and protective competence necessary to a patriarchal family structure disqualifies them from a heroic role. In other Mary Stewart books, where the heroine is not a governess and the plot does not demand a passionate hero, William Blake might have been the hero.

In one important way, all male characters (except for a few recent heroes) resemble each other: they are emotionally remote from the heroines. The hero rarely reveals everything to other people, and he is especially circumspect about emotional matters. He confides in no one. In *Nine Coaches Waiting*, Raoul does not tell Linda about his suspicions of his father, leading her to believe he may himself be a part of the conspiracy. In Stewart's *Airs Above the Ground*, Vanessa suspects her husband of lying to her because she does not know that his so-called business trips cover his work as a secret agent. In Holt's *Bride of Pendorric*, the hero has the answers to most of the questions that trouble his wife, and his failure to explain himself to her makes her suspicious. Series heroes frequently seem to demand that heroines take them on faith as a proof of love. In historical formulas, heroes appear remote because the line between male and female spheres is sharply drawn. Heroes may be offstage when involved in male activities; but even when they are available to women, they rarely reveal their thoughts.

Male emotional reticence provides suspense in the plot, but it also reinforces an assumption of male authority. Even the second male figure knows secrets the heroine can only glimpse; and she depends on him for information, which he reveals on his own internal schedule. The man always unbends at the end to show his love and need for her, but he retains the mastery to be firmly in control of himself and the heroine. His slight thaw convinces the heroine of his love, but it never detracts from his aura of competence and power. In such a hero, love for the heroine represents his vulnerability and reinforces the strength of their bond, reassuring both characters that their love is permanent. Because the hero loves and needs her, the heroine can accept him on faith. And because he values her for herself, submission to him does not require her to give up her own desires. She can, instead, identify with him without fear of disillusion or violation.

Inappropriate men (villains and friends) play roles similar to those of "other women," especially in romantic mysteries, where nonheroic characters may be cast as villains who cannot fit into conventionally domestic relationships. Villains usually fit one of three categories: passionate man, effete man, or "other woman." These patterns underline the implicitly sexual and domestic nature of moral judgments in romances. In all three types of villain, the motive, overtly either greed or jealousy, seems plausible because of the potential for villainy inherent in the character type. Villains have evil natures because they are unfit to play their proper roles in a viable family unit. If their energies were properly channeled into the formation and preservation of a family, they would devote their energies to constructive and productive tasks. The passionate villain may be motivated by greed, but his lack of compassion makes the motive believable, for he does not value sufficiently the love of a virtuous woman. The effete villain may covet beautiful art objects, but in his obsession with them and his complementary devaluation of human relationships he becomes a believable villain. Her beauty betrays the passionate woman, for she attracts men too easily and succumbs to the temptation of yielding to the men who approach her. In squandering her virginity, she fails to develop the complementary female virtues she needs to be admirable.

Romances are adventures for women in the context of changes in family structure over the past two centuries. As the material and social functions of marriage eroded, the family unit became unstable and vulnerable. The nuclear family exists only during the concurrent lives of its members, and the average family lives as a unit (parents and children) for no more than thirty years. Potential instability in the nuclear family has given rise to concern, both articulate and covert, especially since the cohesion for the family is that highly unstable commodity, romantic love. In the family, the member of the group who is able (indeed, required) to function in the outside world is the husband and father. Mother and children depend on him for support and status, and their security rests on his continued sexual interest in his wife. If the husband becomes interested in another woman, or if he turns his energies outward—or if the woman fails to live up to her part of the bargain or fails to perform her domestic roles—the family may collapse. Romances manage and control the threat by portraying heroes with both the power to initiate heroines into adulthood and the perception to value their domesticity. Survival of the patriarchal family depends on both qualities.

Sexual Initiation

In the sexual encounters of romances the relationship between male authority and female redemption of the hero becomes overt. Authors use sex scenes to gauge the quality of the lovers' relationship and to underscore the relative merits of male and female characters. Although the sexual relationship shapes and motivates all romances, until recently sex was covert and euphemistic; even today, sex remains ethereal and emotional, rarely physical or prurient. Before the past decade, however, readers probably derived few vicarious thrills from the elliptical or patently absurd references to intercourse in most romantic biographies and gothic or historical romances. If these books even mention the sex act, they use an allusive language that obscures all physical details. A typical passage from a gothic romance appears in Victoria Holt's *Bride of Pendorric*, shortly after the two characters return from their honeymoon. "Roc was, as I had known he would be, a passionate and demanding lover; he carried me along with him, but I often felt bemused by the rich experiences that were mine."[9] Romance authors describe sex acts through the heroine's *emotions* rather than her physical response, and she *receives* sexual experience from the hero instead of actively participating.

Before the rise of the erotic formula, most romance writers kept the reader at some distance from the physical details of sexuality; the act is suggested, reacted to, mused over, but not explicitly detailed. More recent romances contain much longer and more specific scenes, while continuing to focus on the heroine's emotional response to her lover. Sensuous detail rarely leads to realistic description, and sexuality serves the plot's development instead of dominating it. However, sexuality has always been important in women's romances, despite its covert quality. The tacit agreement between writer and reader suggests that the experience in real life could be only a disappointment after reading the imagined and suggested ecstasies of fiction.

Some writers acknowledge sexuality only when the plot requires an indication of its presence. Mary Stewart, for example, handles sexuality delicately and obliquely, often with humor. She may pass over the issue—as she does when the husband and wife are reunited in *Airs Above the Ground*—with a white space on the page to signify their physical reunion. Although she may acknowledge that lovers feel an erotic attraction, she never dwells on it. In *Touch Not the Cat*, her final novel of romantic suspense, the heroine suddenly realizes her new husband has no more sexual experience than she.

> I went scarlet in my turn, and then suddenly we were both laughing and in each other's arms.
> "Oh, Rob, I just thought you were conventional."
> "What's conventional mean except right? I didn't want it last night because if it was worth waiting for, it was worth waiting till now; and I don't want it now because I don't want it out here in a field with thistles. I want it at home, in bed, and for keeps, on a dark night with no one interrupting. And now you know why."
> "Oh, Rob. Darling Rob . . . I suppose we'll manage somehow. People have."[10]

Stewart does not portray Rob as the experienced initiator nor does Bryony act like the naive, grateful virgin. When she describes their wedding night, she falls back on the euphemisms other romance authors frequently employ, although she acknowledges—in a departure from romance conventions—that Bryony participates instead of merely receiving on her wedding night. Instead of saying "he took me," the heroine says "we took each other."[11]

More conventional wedding night scenes come in two versions: either the heroine's passionate response sweeps her away as she learns to express physical love, or the bestiality and brutality of her husband horrifies her. Georgette Heyer rarely alludes to sex, even when other authors would do so. In *A Civil Contract*, her most explicit scene occurs when the husband in an arranged marriage speaks to his shy bride at the beginning of their honeymoon.

> "But first let me tell you that I'm not blind to the evils of *your* situation. We are barely acquainted, as you have said yourself; it must be very uncomfortable for you indeed!" He smiled at her, not lovingly, but very kindly. "*That* evil will soon be remedied. In the meantime, don't be afraid. I won't do anything you don't like."[12]

End of discussion; end of sex. Barbara Cartland's Regency romances, on the other hand, often discuss sex just before the husband initiates the heroine into her duty and pleasure as his wife, but in a language so inflated and euphemistic that the scenes seem more laughable than plausible. A typical passage occurs in *The Cruel Count*.

"I want to teach you, my adorable perfect sweetheart, about love now that my Sleeping Beauty is awake."

He bent his head and his mouth was very near to hers as he said:

"Have you forgotten that I have to fan that little fire within you into an all-consuming blaze?"

Vesta's lips were almost touching his as she replied:

"It is already . . . burning, darling Miklos."

Then his mouth made her captive, and at his kiss, fierce, passionate, demanding, something wild and incredibly glorious leapt within her.

She felt the ecstasy he evoked in her carrying them both towards the mountain peaks and beyond into a sunlit sky.[13]

Gothic romances rarely contain sex scenes, since the adventurous plots allow authors to avoid explicit portrayals of developing love. However, in some romantic biographies the authors must describe sexual encounters, especially if the book hinges on the irregular sexual relationship of a real woman in the past. When an author includes sex scenes in a romantic biography, she may depict a series of progressive encounters, as Anya Seton does in *Katherine*. The innocent heroine unwillingly marries a boorish knight who only wants her for her beauty. On their wedding night, he consummates the marriage by getting drunk and raping her, and she responds by promising herself that he may own her body but never her soul. "She could surround herself with an impregnable wall of hidden loathing and contempt."[14] Fortunately, he makes few demands on her because he spends much of their marriage fighting battles or recovering from an illness that leaves him impotent. When she encounters John of Gaunt after the death of his first wife, they suddenly recognize their mutual passion and love; but Katherine reminds him that yielding to their desire would be a sin and that they are both still in mourning for his wife. John, like so many other romance heroes, recognizes the signs of her sexual desire before she does; but while

Katherine admits her love and acknowledges that "adultery is so light a thing at court," she refuses him.[15] After her husband's death, however, John comes for her, and Seton describes their initial sexual encounter. "Now there was no need for reticence or gratitude. Here in the sea-scented bedchamber, there was a man and a woman who came together naked and unashamed, proudly bestowing on each other the beauty of their bodies and thereby finding ineffable joy."[16]

Through these progressive scenes, Katherine travels a long way in her sexual attitudes. She begins innocent, virginal, and frightened, holding out against Hugh when she can. She also refuses John's dishonorable offer; but when she, too, is widowed, she feels free to act. Once she has experienced sex with John, she agrees to become his mistress, even though he must remarry for dynastic purposes. John gives Katherine the essence of the romance fantasy: he teaches her about love, sex, and her own reactions; provides a setting for her to play conventional female roles (mother, lover, redeemer); and provides, through their late marriage, the status she deserves.

Even in more sophisticated recent romances, sexual encounters seem ethereal and unrealistic. The heroine is at least emotionally a virgin, and the hero may initiate her verbally before the physical act. Once heroines have found ecstasy, they have no choice but to continue the relationship until death. After Mr. Right, a true woman can be satisfied with nothing less, for sex can never be pleasurable except with the one man the heroine loves. Although she may have other sexual encounters, like Katherine's with her husband, she will never be satisfied by them. Only one man comes along for each woman; and when she finds him, her ecstasy will be total. If she cannot find him or if some impediment to their love cannot be overcome, she faces a lifetime of suffering and loss.

Sexual attraction as the basis for a lasting and fulfilling marriage is crucial to the romance fantasy, most explicitly in recent series and erotic books that use erotic scenes as plot builders, beginning with the first physical encounter and progressing through a series of escalating scenes in which sexual tension rises and must be controlled. In series romances, a typical first encounter occurs when the hero kisses the heroine, often in anger or to prove she responds to him. Her involuntary reaction shocks her because it reveals her vulnerability.

Early sexual encounters are frequently interrupted short of consummation. The hero may stop because he discovers the woman is inexperienced, because he does not want to love her, or because he wants to teach her a lesson about herself. A woman may draw back because she fears sexual relationships, because she is determined to maintain her virginity, because something the hero says brings her to her senses, or because she knows that if she yields she will be irrevocably in love with him. Alternatively, outside agencies intervene: a man's office calls at the crucial moment, a woman's co-worker discovers them, or a crisis occurs. Sexual encounters suggest that erotic impulses can only be controlled through chance or superhuman effort that prevent lovers from consummating their love prematurely. Contemporary romances require conscious control of sexual impulses, for the imperative of sexual attraction would lead to immediate fulfillment unless characters work to control it.

The hero frequently treats the heroine with sympathy and tenderness, once he has her attention. In Kay Thorpe's *The Wilderness Trail*, the hero and heroine are stranded in the Alaskan wilderness. Cal insists that Regan sleep close to him to conserve warmth, and she reluctantly agrees. He kisses her, but she stops him and denies that she desires him. To prove to her that she responds to him, he kisses her again. Cal dominates her through his expertise and experience, but he stops short of consummation because he does not want the responsibility of initiating her into love and adulthood. "You keep your virginity, sweetheart," he tells her. "Some day some man is going to appreciate it. You'll be a quick learner."[17] In his role as authority figure, he proves to her that she has sexual feelings that can be evoked by the right man; in his role as protector, he instructs her about how to conduct herself in the future. The scene identifies Cal as the man who can awaken Regan's sexuality and as a worthy hero to whom she can entrust her future, an irresistible combination.

Although the heroine knows she should resist, the hero's

touch overwhelms her and breaks through her defenses. Heroines leave these encounters shaken by what has occurred and confused by their own responsiveness. But even the more sophisticated romances employ language quite unlike the often deliberately vulgar sexual language of pornography. Romances never use an explicit word when a euphemism can be substituted: a hero's penis is a "male hardness" beneath his clothes or the pressure of his thighs against the woman's body. A heroine's breasts may be described, but her genitals are identified only as the site of a "spreading" or "weakness," or "the center of her heated desire."[18]

The euphemistic language underscores an idealized vision of sexuality and suggests that sexual attraction plays an important, but not exclusive, part in mate selection. A hero can properly initiate the heroine because of his combination of paternal and erotic qualities. A heroine need not worry about money, security, status, or sexual vulnerability if she becomes his wife, for he has the power and maturity to guide her and to ease the impact of the shift from father to lover. He poses few problems of autonomy for her. She does not have to be strong when she is loved by such a man, but his protectiveness allows her to retain her self-respect and the illusion of independence when she submits to him. No matter how domineering and overbearing he may be, when he declares his love for her, submission to him becomes a joy rather than a duty. The heroine admits he was right or forgives him for being wrong. She acknowledges freely that he, alone among men, has the power to stir her emotions and excite her physically. She takes her place as his woman, the one whom he chooses to be in his life.

A hero holds authority but he is not always right. He may have lessons to learn from a woman, although they are rarely so profound as the ones she learns from him. He may be embittered by a loveless childhood and unable to express love until the heroine breaks through his shell. He may have been deeply hurt by another woman and must learn to trust. He may fear, wrongly, that he is too old for the heroine. He may be crippled or maimed and unable to believe that anyone can love him until she convinces him that his problem does not matter to her. A hero may have never loved before and may be unable to recognize at first the value of her love for him. In exchange for sexual initiation and financial and social security for life, she redeems his male rejection of human relationships, introducing him to the meaning of love while he introduces her to its physical expression.

Exploring the Forbidden

Through sex scenes and irregular sexual relationships, romances also explore the forbidden territory of cultural taboo. Earlier formulas used history to distance readers from forbidden expressions of sexuality, especially in royal mistress novels. Contemporary romances, however, frequently dramatize sexual problems or taboo subjects more directly. In Amii Lorin's *The Game Is Played*, the heroine is a thirty-five-year-old gynecologist whose cool, sophisticated, and aloof manner conceals a fear of sex. The hero, Marshall Kirk, five years younger than Helen, abruptly announces he loves her and intends to marry her; although she tries to resist, he will not give up. When he discovers her sexual trauma, he cheerfully agrees to stop pressuring her while insisting she will eventually give in. Marsh is a charming hero—good-looking, self-confident, experienced, understanding, and volatile. Because Helen cannot believe he loves her, she tries to figure out his angle; but her own frozen emotions keep her from recognizing his sincerity. He openly admires her professional work; and when she says she will not "play the three traditional roles" for him, Marsh asks in confusion: "What three roles?" She replies: "The cook in your kitchen, the madonna in your nursery, the mistress in your bed."[19] Marsh tells her he needs and wants none of that, but she cannot believe him.

Marshall Kirk exemplifies the more contemporary hero of the series romance. He differs from the dominant men of earlier novels because he listens to Helen, considers her needs, and expresses his vulnerability—qualities that seem especially appropriate in novels that explore more provocative issues. Another example of the new hero is Kai Ellington in Karen van der Zee's *A Secret Sorrow*. Kai does not conceal his emotions from the heroine, and he admits his love for her early in the book. Faye, however, resists his declaration because she cannot have children, and she knows Kai wants a family. Ashamed of her perceived failure, she finds it impossible to tell him the truth. Kai reveals explicit vulnerability as he pleads for an explanation of her refusal to marry him. When he learns the truth, it upsets him at first; but he quickly gains control of himself and tells her she had no right to keep the problem to herself. Because they share the dilemma, they will face it together.

Kai, in contrast to some other heroes, does not try to dominate the heroine; he offers her sympathy, understanding, and the authority to help her accept her personal tragedy. Unlike some romance heroes, who may demand children as heirs or extensions of themselves, Kai seems as nurturing and loving as Faye in scenes where he cares for the heroine's motherless niece and nephew. In his sensitivity, understanding, and ability to express and give love, Kai represents a significant change in series heroes. Confident of himself, he still poses no threat of domination to the heroine.

Incest, a stronger and more deeply rooted cultural taboo than the age disparity and sexual trauma of *The Game Is Played* or the sterility of *A Secret Sorrow*, underlies romances with love relationships between stepsisters and stepbrothers. These characters have been raised in the same household, although the hero is frequently years older than the heroine, and he may have acted as a surrogate father for his younger "sister." They may, as in Amii Lorin's *The Tawny Gold Man*, acknowledge their romantic feelings too early, before the heroine gains the maturity for sexual initiation. The characters spend ten years apart while the heroine grows up. In Brooke Hastings's *Island Conquest*, an early sexual encounter (unconsummated) leads to years of conflict before the characters marry. Siblings share many similar experiences and have a rapport that may be absent between potential lovers of disparate backgrounds. They live in close proximity and have opportunities for illicit encounters denied to other lovers. In the eyes of the world, they are inappropriate partners for each other; but in romances with this theme, the taboo can be transcended. As relatives without blood ties, they are not legally prohibited from marriage. Their attraction for each other may verge on scandal, but no intrinsic barriers of consanguinity separate them. Their triumph asserts, against a censorious world, the power of true love, for they work through the barriers of the incest taboo without violating it.

Although the impediments to love in stepbrother romances may be similar to those of other books, the additional issue of the characters' sibling relationship reinforces the developmental significance of the courtship fantasy. If the easing of the patriarchal transition from father to husband is a central problem for women, a stepbrother (especially a much older one) offers an attractive option for the heroine of a romance. Through proximity, he knows her well, and he has often had a hand in guiding her through childhood and adolescence. He knows her faults and apparently does not hold them against her. He shares with her a set of circumstances—background, family experience, goals, and beliefs—that promises to control and ease the problems of adulthood because she need not change to accommodate her membership in a new family. He offers her the security of familiarity and the excitement of an apparently forbidden romance. The wedding night scene of *Island Conquest* demonstrates the pattern. The heroine emerges apprehensively in her nightgown to find that her new husband also appears reticent. She taunts him: "What's the matter, Daniel? Afraid of losing your virginity?" He responds, almost paternally: "No. . . . Nervous about taking yours. Afraid of hurting you."[20] Stepbrothers, like fathers, are protective and adoring; and the future holds little to fear if the heroine's husband deserves the same trust and love as her father.

Waiting to Be Chosen

Through their climactic scenes, the final few pages when the characters acknowledge their love, romances offer a vicarious fantasy or recapitulation of the exquisite moment of being chosen. In the reconciliation between lovers, the hero's authority is crucial, for a heroine may be oblivious to the signs of love. She may understand neither her own feelings nor those of the hero, and her acknowledgment may depend on his perception as he instructs her to recognize the truth. In Georgette Heyer's *Frederica*, the hero teaches the heroine the nature of love when he proposes to her. Frederica says she has not thought about marrying him. Alverstoke says, ruefully, that he knows that. She suggests that he thinks he compromised her when they spent time together without a chaperone; he denies it. She tells him that he does not want to marry her; he agrees, adding that since everyone apparently believes he will, he will be humiliated if she rejects him. She says that she has to take care of her two young brothers, and he says he wants to help. When she accuses him of marrying her out of compassion, he again demurs. Finally, she says that she cannot believe he loves her.

"Oh, not in the least," he assured her cheerfully. "It is merely that I find I cannot live without you, my adorable Frederica!"

"Is it like *that*? Being in love? You see, I never was in love, so I don't know. . . . It has always seemed to me that if one falls in love with any gentleman one becomes instantly blind to his faults. But I am *not* blind to your faults, and I do *not* think that everything you do or say is right! Only—Is it being—not very comfortable—and cross—and not quite *happy*, when you aren't there?"

"That, my darling," said his lordship, taking her ruthlessly into his arms, "is *exactly* what it is!"

"Oh—!" Frederica gasped, as she emerged from an embrace which threatened to suffocate her. "*Now* I know! I am in love!"[21]

Alverstoke seems less authoritarian than some other romance heroes because he does not know how Frederica feels, but he has enough authority to define love for her and to give her the information she requires to respond properly to his proposal. Male knowledge and authority in matters of love are constants in romance fiction; but, paradoxically, expertise in human relationships belongs to woman's sphere. Conventionally, in the act of being chosen—when the hero makes his declaration—a woman knows she has earned the right to take on the responsibilities inherent in her intuitive expertise. He bears the responsibility of making the choice before she can perform her womanly duties.

The implications of waiting to be chosen pose serious difficulties, both for women in fiction and for women in real life. Women must prepare themselves for love and marriage, but they must wait for the hero to speak first. Because women read men's minds in fiction much less well than the reverse, the declaration may come as a shock; and the heroine may not believe him. Outside issues—the opinion of the world, money, family responsibilities, moral questions, appropriateness of time and place—affect a heroine's ability to discern what she actually wants.

In romances, the recognition of love represents the recognition of the female self, binding closer together the resolution of problems between lovers and the assumption of true female identity. Women in romances appear to be self-deceived. They often do not know what they want until they are told by the hero, who offers both love and adult identity in the same package. Additionally, because of the double standard, women feel less free to engage in premarital sex, so they must make blind decisions about the future. Men, on the other hand, are free—in fact, often expected—to experiment through illicit liaisons. As heroines negotiate the course of love, they must be wary of false trails and immoral acts that would forever banish them to failure. A premature "yes" is just as threatening as a mistaken "no," for each leads potentially to disaster.

Sex in romances resembles the sexual attitudes described by pioneer researchers William Masters and Virginia H. Johnson, who conducted the first sustained clinical and psychological studies of the process of sex in a cultural context, unlike the earlier Kinsey reports that were based on interviews rather than observation. The first Masters and Johnson volumes were deliberately technical, written for scientists out of a concern that the general public might be scandalized by their research methods. Although there was controversy, especially about the research that employed surrogate wives for sexually inadequate men, the studies immediately achieved a wide audience. Later, they publicized their findings through magazine articles and in a 1974 book entitled *The Pleasure Bond: A New Look at Sexuality and Commitment.*

Masters and Johnson delineate three stages of development

in the social mythology of sexuality. In Stage I, sex is done by the male *to* the female. In Stage II, it is done by the male *for* the female. In Stage III, their ideal if elusive goal, it is performed by the male *with* the female. These stages have historical roots, and they chart changes in the ideology of sexuality as it affects the social consequences of sexual practice.

Masters and Johnson locate Stage I historically in the separation of sex roles that occurred during the industrial revolution. Sexuality was repressed, denied status as a natural function, regarded as shameful, and regulated by society. The double standard ordained the man as "sex expert."[22] For more than two centuries, the researchers suggest, men carried responsibility for the sex act, and they had to know what to do to their partners. Women, however, were assumed to be both ignorant and sexually unresponsive. "Everyone knew—or at least all men knew and most women pretended—that 'nice' women had no sexual feelings, that respected wives only submitted in the hope of conceiving and that 'those women' who freely responded sexually weren't the kind you married."[23] This attitude toward female sexuality informs the value patterns of early romances, beginning with seduction stories and continuing into this century. Sexual emotions were confined either to the trauma of the wedding night, when a man had to know how to be gentle and the woman quaked timidly, or to the euphemistically described yearnings of women outside the bounds of respectability.

Stage II, Masters and Johnson suggest, was a side effect of publicity about the Kinsey research, which freed women to admit that sex was not painful or traumatic and that they experienced desire. As a result, public attitudes began to acknowledge "that women not only had real sexual feelings and legitimate sexual interest, but also could and should be orgasmic—something that millions of women (even 'nice' women) could have revealed had they ever been asked and been assured that their answers would have been accepted without being judged."[24] The responsibility for sexual satisfaction, however, continued to rest with the male, who added to his role as expert the additional duty of satisfying his wife. This Stage II attitude toward sex as a service performed *by* the male *for* the female remains the dominant mode of romances today.

Masters and Johnson discovered that in many sexually incompatible couples the wife seeks help and assumes voluntarily the role of problem.[25] When a man assumes the role of expert, a woman believes she must be at fault if she fails to learn from him. The attitude jeopardizes effective sexual relationships, they believe, because the woman fails to take responsibility for a pleasurable relationship, and the man cannot do it alone. The cultural message has changed inevitably, allowing women greater freedom to express themselves sexually, but it still imposes on the man responsibilities and expertise that few can maintain.

Stage III, according to Masters and Johnson, obtains among only a minority of couples. "Effective sexual functioning is something that transpires between two people. To be effective it must be done together. It is something that sexually functional couples do *with* each other, not *to* or *for* each other."[26] Masters and Johnson imply that sex removed from the realm of natural function becomes covert, problematic, and troublesome for both men and women. The requirements for sex in Stages I and II are rigid; and although the recognition that women have sexual responses is a move in the right direction, it imposes its own tyranny. The treatment of sex in most romances embodies the Stage II assumption that men *give* and women *respond*. But the novels hedge sex with restrictions that allow it to occur only within a monogamous value system. Romance heroines are conventionally unresponsive to sex without love, unlike heroes, who may split emotion from its physical expression in relationships before marriage.

Romances before the mid-twentieth century either ignored sex and sexuality entirely or portrayed sexual relations in Stage I—sex was done *by* a man *to* a woman—with virtually no indication that a woman could either actively participate or enjoy it. When romances began to portray sexuality more frequently, Stage II attitudes dominated, and since the 1950s, most novels reinforce the Stage II pattern. Even heroines who openly admit their enjoyment of sex (with Mr. Right) often hesitate to initiate an encounter. As in other aspects of courtship, heroines wait passively to be chosen sexually. The hero teaches, gives, and acts; and his explicit value as a hero in a romance derives from his ability to initiate and satisfy her. Masters and Johnson ascribe to this attitude many of the problems in modern marriages, but in the romance fantasy it is the ideal. Women socialized to passivity in sexual relationships might have great difficulty in identifying with fictional characters who do not share their values, although they may find vicarious pleasure in identifying with fictional women who have sexual experience beyond their own. Women are conditioned to see sex and love as identical, and the freedom to respond does not confer the freedom to be aggressive in initiating sex.

Romances, however, evade real-life problems by depicting a world in which they are irrelevant, for heroines invariably find sexual fulfillment simultaneously with love. The hero confers two rewards on the heroine: sexual initiation and the opportunity to perform traditional roles for him. The existence of this attitude in romances confirms Masters and Johnson's view of the factors inhibiting Stage III. If Stage I attitudes have declined, Stage II poses its own problems for effective sexual functioning. Surely, the contemporary popularity of sex manuals reflects widespread social discontent with prevailing patterns of sexual expression. The idealized sexuality of romances undoubtedly maintains socialized reality for some women, just as some men find reassurance in the myth of male mastery common to pornography.

If Masters and Johnson's analysis of culturally accepted attitudes accurately reflects the sexual beliefs of our culture, the portrayal of male authority in romances undoubtedly works to assuage uncomfortable perceptions for many women. The hegemony of Stage II places burdens on both partners: on the male because he is responsible for the sexual response of both and on the female because it becomes her fault if she cannot respond properly despite his expertise. A woman need not deny her sexual impulses, but she still expects to respond to male authority. Ideally, the regulation of sexuality occurs through the institution of monogamous marriage. Thus, sexual expression and marriage both depend on male assertiveness and female passivity. Romances dramatize a fantasy in which women do not have to take responsibility for initiating sexual relationships, although they play a significant role in controlling them. Without taking the initiative or putting themselves at risk, readers experience sexuality vicariously by identifying with heroines who share their dilemmas, inhibitions, and values but whose sexual adventures may far surpass their own.

Social behavior is undoubtedly more liberal than romance conventions, but actual changes in sexual practice occur only by accretion and over long periods of time. No wonder millions of readers who came to maturity between 1950 and 1975 turn to romances for models when they perceive disquieting distinctions between their socialized beliefs and their observations of the changing world around them. Contemporary romances allow readers to have it both ways. They acknowledge a woman's sexual responsiveness by making it a crucial factor in identifying the hero. They portray sexual encounters as a transcendent experience that remains subject to control in traditional modes. They acknowledge male expertise by granting it to a hero who combines sexual knowledge with love for the heroine. And they grant to women the power to domesticate these powerful figures through heroines who conform to cultural expectations of female passivity. For women facing the impact of the sexual revolution but unable—for whatever reason—to participate in it, or for those unsatisfied by their own experience, the euphemistic eroticism of women's romances might bring a vicarious pleasure denied in their own lives.

Sexuality remains a sensitive area for many women, despite publicized alterations in social practice. If women yearn for marriage, they can fantasize a perfect relationship through reading. If they are already married, they can ameliorate perceptions of discontent through vicarious participation in a better relationship. Vicarious experience may seem especially desirable in this instance, because in few areas of male-female relationships does the risk of change appear so great. Certainly premarital sex carries less stigma today, and a woman may feel free to admit that she finds sex pleasurable. But cultural ideology does not change so rapidly as sexual practice, and the profound tensions of cultural evolution are imperfectly mirrored in romances. Vicarious sexual experience through the romance fantasy allows readers, especially in an area they may find difficult to discuss openly, to deny any uncomfortable feelings and insist that proper behavior leads to fulfillment. Romances, like other formulas, respond to a conservative urge to have adventure without risk.

The emergence of erotic romances after more than two centuries of tamer formulas illuminates the fantasy's significance, for erotic romances allow depiction of acts and attitudes long proscribed in romances, while continuing to locate sexual experience in a romantic context. As women socialized to Stage II expectations began to reach maturity, the romance fantasy altered to allow readers to explore forbidden—and perhaps frightening—possibilities in private, without the need to act or take risks.

But fictional formulas always remain bound to their cultural context, and in their response to social change they frequently reveal the inherent difficulties in challenging social mythology. Certainly, romance formulas have changed in the past decade—especially in premarital sex and more vulnerable heroes—but the persistent pattern of male authority and female passivity suggests that these alterations may be less substantial than they appear on the surface. If women continue to remain dependent on men for portions of their adult identity—to wait to be chosen—the romance fantasy may incorporate more flexible conventions without undermining its basic premise. Romances, like all formulas, perform a conservative function. It will, no doubt, take more than a few years of sexual revolution and feminist challenge for many women to become the judges of their own lives.

Notes

1. Jayne Castle, *Gentle Pirate* (New York: Dell, 1980), 67–68.
2. Ian Watt, *The Rise of the Novel* (Berkeley: Univ. of California Press, 1957), 153–54.
3. Mary Stewart, *Nine Coaches Waiting* (Greenwich, Conn.: Fawcett Crest, 1958), 146–47.
4. Ibid., 271.
5. Ibid.

6. Lowry Nelson, Jr., "Night Thoughts on the Gothic Novel," *Yale Review* 52 (1962): 250.

7. Barbara Cartland, *A Halo for the Devil* (New York: Pyramid, 1972), 15–16.

8. Mary Stewart, *My Brother Michael* (Greenwich, Conn.: Fawcett Crest, 1959), 40–41.

9. Victoria Holt, *Bride of Pendorric* (Greenwich, Conn.: Fawcett Crest, 1963), 21.

10. Mary Stewart, *Touch Not the Cat* (New York: Fawcett Crest, 1976), 246.

11. Ibid., 291.

12. Georgette Heyer, *A Civil Contract* (New York: Ace, 1961), 94.

13. Barbara Cartland, *The Cruel Count* (London: Pan Books, 1974), 184.

14. Anya Seton, *Katherine* (Greenwich, Conn.: Fawcett Crest, 1954), 111.

15. Ibid., 231.

16. Ibid., 292.

17. Kay Thorpe, *The Wilderness Trail* (Toronto: Harlequin Books, 1979), 62.

18. Castle, *Gentle Pirate*, 178.

19. Amii Lorin, *The Game Is Played* (New York: Dell, 1981), 177.

20. Brooke Hastings, *Island Conquest* (New York: Silhouette Books, 1981), 183.

21. Georgette Heyer, *Frederica* (New York: Avon, 1965), 348–50.

22. William Masters and Virginia H. Johnson, *The Pleasure Bond: A New Look at Sexuality and Commitment* (Boston: Little Brown, 1974), 3.

23. Ibid., 3–4.

24. Ibid., 5.

25. Ibid., 8.

26. Ibid., 7.

6

The Dynamic of Romance Formulas

Dear Friend:

This letter was started by a woman like yourself in the hope of bringing relief to other tired and discontented women. Unlike most chain letters, this one does not cost anything. Just send a copy of this letter to five of your friends who are equally discontented. Then, bundle up your husband or boy friend and send him to the woman whose name appears at the top of the list and add your name to the bottom of the list.

When your name comes to the top of the list, you will receive 16,877 men and one of them is bound to be a lot better than the one you already have!

DO NOT BREAK THE CHAIN . . . . HAVE FAITH! One woman broke the chain and got her own S.O.B. back. We're counting on you!

Washington Post Magazine
23 August 1981

Romances require conventional elements familiar to readers, but conventions—settings, characters, situations—only set the stage. The dynamic of romances—John Cawelti calls it the "pattern of action"—shapes their meaning for the audience. The dynamic of the romance fantasy is flexible enough to incorporate changing social conditions over time, and those changes relate to psychosocial tensions within female socialization patterns and serve as a measure of feminine consciousness in a patriarchal society.

Fictional formulas respond to individual needs produced by culture, and they reconcile individual readers to their cultural roles and beliefs. In *The Social Construction of Reality*, Peter L. Berger and Thomas Luckmann argue that cultures define, inculcate, and maintain a vision of reality for their members; and those constructions of reality work in specific and describable ways. Cultures employ a variety of techniques to socialize members into a common vision of the real world; and because the socialized vision shapes a collective consciousness, individuals only rarely question—or even try to identify—the most basic beliefs that they share with others. Socially constructed beliefs are so massive and simply taken for granted that they defy articulation.[1] In addition, understanding the origin and rationale for these beliefs requires more effort than apprehending their consequences. In attempting to describe the way things are, individuals in culture often rely on stereotypical statements that both reaffirm and perpetuate existing conditions and beliefs.

The popular arts play a part in the process of socialization, for they assert, support, and demonstrate the rightness of the underlying belief structure of a culture. Popular arts are conservative in intent and conception. They do not exactly reflect a culture—they are, after all, products of its fantasies—but they do validate it by supporting the inherent values mutually agreed on a priori by individuals. These values and assumptions become reality because the culture presents no acceptable alternatives. Popular formulas are fantasies; but escape into fantasy is not simplistic, for formulas offer their readers a complex vicarious world that reaffirms belief patterns and ameliorates the tensions arising between an individual's participation in culture and her perceptions of herself and her feelings.

The desire for escape from the perceived frustrations of socialized reality may be as old as culture itself, although the object of the escape changes over time. Many forms of cultural expression provide escape. Ritualized competition, for example, offers a way for participants and audience alike to involve themselves in tests of individual strength and to assert control over the precariousness of daily existence. A culture's myths and legends similarly manage fears and tensions engendered in individuals by cultural prescriptions and challenges. Escape has a paradoxical quality only apprehended through an understanding of its dynamic, for any mechanism of escape must be repetitive to be effective. Individuals ordinarily choose multiple versions of the story or game because its pleasure is temporary.

In addition, effective escape mechanisms are widely disseminated in a culture, and they may be largely unconscious, because the conditions to which they respond, like all social myths, seem so obvious that they defy articulation. Most readers of escape fiction—like compulsive television viewers or sports fans—find it difficult to describe the motives that lead them to seek one form of escape over another. If escape ameliorates tensions that remain largely covert and unexamined, then attempting to explain the attraction of a particular escape mechanism might negate its value. John Cawelti's assertion that the most successful formulas appeal to a wide range of possible audiences suggests that simple answers—"the six-gun is a phallic symbol for frustrated males," "romances are rape fantasies"—do not tell the whole story.

Romances rarely satisfy us as art, for their aesthetics differs from the appeal we ascribe to serious fiction—the ability of an original work of art to extend and deepen our understanding of the human condition. Instead, fictional formulas offer variations on a theme by acting simultaneously as a psychosocial release valve for frustrations and a tranquilizer that reconciles those competing beliefs, attitudes, and desires that remain problematic in everyday life. In their resolution of psychosocial tensions, popular formulas reaffirm social myths, constructions of reality that explain and reconcile phenomena to the ideal on both individual and collective levels. Myths embody collective beliefs that allow individuals in culture to communicate, to act, and to relate to one another.

Popular culture disseminates and manages the social myths of a culture, reassuring the reader or audience that, at least in the world of fantasy (that can be obtained at will), socialized values remain both functional and true. Myths embody the commonsense knowledge that most members of society agree to be true (or relevant), act on, and employ to explain experience; and their values reflect conventional problems and solutions sanctified by the social organization of culture. Repetitive reading of formula fiction allows readers to assert temporary, vicarious control over tensions and anxieties that might otherwise threaten to undermine the fabric of cultural socialization.

A formula's dynamic derives from its dual role as entertainment and reassurance and from its differential appeal to members of a heterogeneous audience. As both entertainment and reassurance, each reading experience temporarily relieves certain anxieties within the reader by taking her out of the contradictions of the real world and allowing vicarious participation in a more rationally structured fantasy. The transitory experience ends on the last page of each novel, but a reader can repeat it by choosing another book. Because popular fiction relates to culture's conservative function, its unrealistic and shallow solutions fail to provide genuine answers for complex collective problems.

The fictional world contains situations and problems related to the reader's world and more exciting and difficult than her own, but it does not require of her either positive action or a reorganization of her belief system. A reader experiences the fictional world without taking responsibility for its implications, because vicarious fantasy has the power to transform tension and frustration into manageable patterns that can be experienced as pleasurable. As a mass, readers seek fictional escape from frustrating and anxious lives; but the goal of escape differs from group to group and, indeed, from reader to reader. If a reader finds gratification in a particular formula, the significant issues concern the reasons for her response and the complex formulaic patterns that produce gratification for large numbers of individual readers.

The persistence of formulas among members of specific groups suggests that mere distraction must be accompanied by genuine involvement in the object of escape. The need for escape may be a psychological fact of life for all members of a culture, and members of identifiable demographic groups may seek similar types of vicarious experience; but the reading of formula fiction relates to both the psychological organization of individual consciousness and the exigencies of society. Fictional formulas are, after all, highly structured ways of perceiving the world.

Fantasy and the Reading Experience

As fantasies, romances share characteristics with other fantasies, literary or nonliterary. The human urge to tell stories—to imagine situations alien to actual circumstances—derives from the human ability to plan, to imagine events that may happen, just as it allows us to enjoy stories of events that may or may not have happened to others. Storytelling opens infinite possibilities and offers an alternative vision through imagining or hearing the experiences of others. Stories, even true ones, are fantasies in the minds of those who hear them. At its most mythic, storytelling creates and disseminates shared cultural explanations of reality. At its best, fantasy offers a mind-expanding and liberating experience; however, it can also represent an obsessive reworking of past decisions and missed opportunities. It is rooted in human language in the phrases "If I could only . . . " and "If I had only . . . " The conditional quality recognizes that human beings have some freedom of choice and responsibility for the choices they make, especially when a decision—for example, marriage—is difficult to revoke.

Eric Klinger's *Structure and Functions of Fantasy*, a psychological study of daydreams, suggests a framework for understanding the power of the romance fantasy. A novel, of course, differs from a daydream because the author, not the reader, retains control of its shape and content. In a daydream, a woman imagines within the limits of her own invention; but daydreams are limited by the conditions of an individual's life, while fiction allows a reader to try on an alternate identity through identification with a character. Fiction takes readers out of the conditions of their own lives and into the world of another—the character with whom they most closely identify—but it imposes a set of limits, for the events of the story are limited to the author's vision and the author's plot. Readers do not normally fantasize outside these limits; so the free play of the imagination is partially suppressed, even though different readers undoubtedly read the same book in different ways, each responding to the aspects that most appeal to specific tensions and needs. And yet, Klinger's work on daydreams contains significant analogies to the profiles of readers who choose romances.

Klinger reports that daydreaming begins at the point in the life cycle when active children's play ends, that it peaks in late adolescence and early adulthood, and then declines slowly.[2] These daydreams, from prepubescence through early adulthood, are more prospective than retrospective; and as they decline in adulthood, the proportion changes progressively. Fantasies in adolescence seem to anticipate "possible future developments in the subject's life in the areas of vocation, achievement, athletics, and sex," while in adulthood, daydreams deal increasingly with past life situations rather than with the future.[3] Klinger cites a 1968 study that "argues convincingly that the decline of prospective fantasy reflects the realistic closing of major life options."[4] Significantly, however, such daydreams decline rather than cease.

Klinger's profile of daydreams reflects common sense; individuals growing older and facing the closing of life options undoubtedly turn more frequently to fantasies of "what might have been" than to fantasies of "what might be." More significantly, however, Klinger's formulation parallels the readership profiles of the Mann surveys and the Yankelovich, Skelly, and White study that show reading reaching a peak in the middle years and declining slowly as individuals grow old.[5] Fictional fantasy seems most important in the life cycle at a later stage than daydreams. Daydreams, controlled by individuals, dominate when life options are open—or appear to be so—while reading, controlled externally, increases when many options have already concluded or passed. As it becomes increasingly difficult to daydream—to imagine open situations where free choice seems possible—the controlled fantasy of fiction assumes more importance, allowing readers to try on new identities by imagining themselves in new situations with new possibilities as an experiment in different life experiences and modes of achievement. Both daydreams and reading, however, are private processes during which individuals may imagine experiences they might hesitate to confront openly.

Norman Holland, in *The Dynamics of Literary Response*, suggests that readers do not project themselves into a fictional situation or imagine themselves as actors in the fantasy. Instead, readers engage in the "willing suspension of disbelief" by introjecting the fantasy into their own mental processes, by taking the world of the fiction into the self through internalization.[6] Reading does not require a woman to take risks or leaps into the unknown; instead she allows the fantasy to consume her consciousness for a specific, limited period of time. Holland argues that reading, like dreaming, involves regression into an earlier, oral state of "being-in-the-world" as the reader absorbs the fantasy into the self. One part of the conscious mind experiences the fantasy as if it were immediate while, on another level of consciousness, the reader continues to engage in mature reality-testing in judgments of the fiction's plausibility and content, thus keeping herself distant and detached from the fantasy experience.[7] Regression lets the reader off the hook of having to act or change while still allowing her to confront painful or forbidden issues in a manageable form.

A reader does not identify with a work by desiring to be someone else, Holland suggests; to the contrary, she takes into herself the entirety of a protagonist's life history and circumstances as a temporary substitute for her own. Reading enlarges life by providing possibilities for experiencing alternate states, prospective or retrospective; it may offer another experience outside the range of one's own life or make it possible to retain prospective fantasies beyond the point when they can be spontaneously self-generated.

In effect, the literary work dreams a dream for us. It embodies and evokes in us a central fantasy; then it manages and controls that fantasy by devices that, were they in a mind, we would call defenses, but, being on a page, we call "form." And the having of the fantasy and feeling it managed gives us pleasure.[8]

Outright romantic daydreams about romance may be characteristic of young women imagining what is in store for them, but such fantasies might be less acceptable to older women. If challenging social mythology makes individuals uncomfortable, reading offers a safe outlet for frustrations and doubts. Older women may have achieved marriage, but they may have become disillusioned because it fails to live up to their expectations. They may fear they will never have an opportunity to fulfill their most cherished dreams. However, a married woman might be inhibited, even privately, in imagining herself in a romantic situation, especially if she finds it uncomfortable to find an acceptable way of disposing of her husband before the daydream can proceed. Romantic fantasies for a married woman might be more acceptable when she tries on a vicarious identity that neatly sidesteps the encumbering realities of husband, family, home, and life circumstances. Of course, unmarried women also read romances; and not all married women who read romances do so for these reasons and in precisely this way.

Achieving Adult Identity

If fiction, especially escape fiction, does work in this way—providing a safe and satisfying way for readers to imagine themselves in new situations with different life circumstances, problems, and choices—then the courtship fantasy of romances assumes more concrete outlines for analysis. Many psychologists agree that women continue to define themselves in the context of family relationships, whether researchers attribute the phenomenon to innate traits or to cultural factors in women's environment. Theories of psychosexual development, for example, place great emphasis on the passage of a woman from adolescence to adulthood, the process of transition in a patriarchal society from father to husband. The significance of that passage in a woman's life is a constantly reiterated baseline of female development in psychoanalytic and psychosocial models. But one does not have to participate in Freudian controversies to believe that, for some women, adult identity hinges on establishing a mature relationship with a man. The cultural evidence lies all around us in social myth and in the purely practical details of everyday life.

Despite the inadequacy of Freud's formulations of female psychosexual development—and beyond the as-yet-unanswered question of innate sexual differences—psychoanalytic theory offers a way of putting these issues into a manageable perspective while also suggesting the significance of mate selection and family formation for women in our culture. Freud suggests that a girl is first actively attached to her mother and, like a boy, fantasizes about possessing her. Learning that this is a physical impossibility, the girl transfers her attention to her father, but she does not need to repress her attraction to her mother as does her brother, nor does she need to compete with her father to mature. Instead, she finds acceptable her attachment to the parent of the opposite sex, which ameliorates the problem of a later shift in allegiance to another male, her husband. Her maturation depends on competition with other women for the father's attention rather than competition with him for dominance. Unlike a boy, her choice of a lover is not a "fundamental shift in the girl's sexuality," but a further stage in its development.[9] In the shift from mother to father, a female accepts a passive role that requires her to wait to be chosen or noticed by the male. In a patriarchal society, a woman learns to be her father's daughter and her husband's wife—and a mother to children. The very acceptance of these dependent, reflected relationships predisposes a woman to a surface passivity in her choice of the mate through whom she gains adult identity. Ironically, this ideal of passivity—waiting to be chosen—remains strong even though mate selection is a crucial factor in a woman's adult status and identity.

Erik Erikson identifies as the crucial stage in a woman's development the relinquishing of her birth family and commitment to the "stranger," her husband.[10] According to Julia Sherman, Erikson believes "identity for a woman is formed and expresses itself in the selective nature of her search for the kind of man by whom she wishes to be sought."[11] Joyce Ladner's analysis of thirty lower-class adolescent girls led her to conclude that the "transition from virgin to non-virgin is the most crucial stage of psychosexual development" because she found such strikingly distinct characteristics in comparing the two groups. "The virgins were more immature, obedient to parental authority, and held strong beliefs about morality. They tended to romanticize relations with their boyfriends."[12] These are almost precisely the qualities of many romance heroines, even those with sexual experience.

Nancy Chodorow, in *The Reproduction of Mothering*, argues that Freud approaches female development from a stance of cultural prejudice rather than through the modes of clinical description he employed to analyze the male. By constantly defining woman as "the other"—the "not male"—Freud and many of his followers (as well as his critics, to be sure) failed to *observe* female development in itself and instead described it against the baseline of male patterns. Thus, cultural attitudes about the inferiority of women became the source of Freud's assertion of the role of "penis envy" in the female.[13] Karen Horney replaced "penis envy" with an innate female urge to mother, a more complex formulation of motivation, perhaps, but no less problematic. Chodorow's account of female psychosexual development places less emphasis than do some others on inherent and innate qualities, but she also finds family formation and mate selection significant in the female life cycle.

Chodorow argues that women *do* make the shift from identification with the mother to the father, experiencing a measure of hostility to the mother in the oedipal stage. They *do* go on in normal heterosexual development to transfer their allegiance from father to husband at that crucial point in their lives, and the identification with their husbands confers both status and the opportunity to perform traditional female roles in families of their own. But Chodorow suggests that the nature of female attachment to others differs from the male model; instead of rejecting her mother, the girl attaches herself to her father by enlarging the number of persons with whom she actively affiliates, and her choice of marriage partner enlarges that circle once more, as does her bearing of children.[14]

Chodorow's description seems remarkably similar to the actions of many heroines in romances, for it combines both aspects of the romance dynamic: the love story and the domestic test. Without totally rejecting previous attachments, women in romances gather around them others who allow them to perform traditional roles. Romances evade the uncomfortable implications of the oedipal struggle by displacing anxiety through an idealized portrayal of femininity confirmed by male authority. The romantic bond provides the cultural context for a woman to replicate her mother's functions, and it offers an acceptable mode for her to act out her libidinous heterosexual self and avoid incest.

Carol Gilligan's *In a Different Voice* illuminates the romance fantasy in her description of the differing modes of thought when men and women confront common moral problems. Beginning like Chodorow with the assumption that psychological development theories define men as the norm and women as deviant, Gilligan demonstrates that women's decision-making strategies favor concern for the value of human relationships over reliance on abstract concepts of rights, justice, or logic. When measured on the Thematic Apperception Test, for example, college men perceived potential violence in pictures that implied intimacy or touching, but women feared dangerous consequences from scenes suggesting achievement or competition. When presented with a picture of trapeze artists gripping each other in mutual support, men described situations of betrayal and revenge while some women provided a safety net for protection.

As people are brought closer together in the pictures, the images of violence in the men's stories increase, while as people are set further apart, the violence in women's stories increases. The women in the class projected violence most frequently into the picture of the man at his desk (the only picture portraying a person alone), while the men in the class most often saw violence in the scene of the acrobats on the trapeze (the only picture in which people touched). Thus, it appears that men and women may experience attachment and separation in different ways and that each sex perceives a danger which the other does not see—men in connection and women in separation.[15]

If women seek attachment and fear isolation, the suspense of a love story offers a congenial fantasy, for romances manage the fear that the heroine will be left alone and defeated because the lovers failed to work out their problems and find mutual commitment. If successful courtship confers adult identity on women in culture, then fantasies about that moment might ameliorate some tensions produced by unrealistic expectations. Even in the most adventurous romances, the danger (or crime) is directed at a domestic circle that must be preserved by the heroine. Her reward is marriage, the female attachment that usually occurs in young adulthood when a woman shifts her identity from her father and commits herself to her husband.

Romances also ameliorate the inherent frustrations of female adulthood, for they reinforce and maintain the significance of a woman's sphere. As women assume adult status in society, they accept the traditional social roles they will perform as the way things must be. For women, achievement motivations often must give way to the competing need to affiliate with others, for most women learn to value themselves through external approval. The nature of oedipal conflict between father and son encourages men to develop a coherent sense of self, while for women validation takes place through interpersonal relationships. Juanita H. Williams clarifies the developmental significance of female ambivalence about achievement and affiliation.

The culture prompts her very early to become sensitive to the responses of others, and to evaluate herself accordingly. She learns to be and to behave in ways that will maximize for her the powerful reward of love, admiration, and approval. But to the extent that her self-esteem and sense of self become dependent upon such rewards, she is dependent upon the presence of significant others for their delivery, and she fails to develop internal criteria for an evaluation and definition of her self. Thus, she remains tentative in outline so that she may adapt more easily to the man she marries whose personality is as yet unknown.

. . . .

Because successful achievement threatens to interfere with or to preclude successful affiliation leading to identity and performance as wife and mother, any serious contemplation of it as a major part of one's life style is productive of anxiety and avoidance. The threat consists of two major obstacles, the evidence for which is all around her. First, if her successful achievement is unfeminine, then men will not find her desirable, and second, high achievement calls for difficult preparation and sustained effort, which may require deferral of affiliative goals.[16]

Matina Horner's influential studies of the "motive to avoid success" in college women suggest that the conflict between achievement and affiliation carries a high price tag for young women who

accept society's attitudes and then tend to evaluate themselves in terms of these attitudes which stress the idea that competition, success, competence, and intellectual achievement are basically inconsistent with femininity. The emphasis on the new freedom of women has not done away with this tendency, anymore than have the vote, trousers, cigarettes, and even similar standards of sexual behavior.[17]

Women who fear negative consequences from success, however, may respond by experiencing "frustration, hostility, aggression, bitterness, and confusion."[18]

Competing imperatives also affect married women. In the very performance of the traditional female roles—wife, mother, and homemaker—there are inherent tensions, fears of failure, and instability that may cause problems for individual women. Women can feel fragmented and unimportant because of the unfocused nature of their activities. They face a built-in obsolescence because their roles depend on a highly specified number of significant others who can and do leave them. They are encouraged to expend their energies and identification on unstable relationships, while considering personal career development, for example, as merely a contingency plan. They may find threatening any attempt to combine female roles with a career, for the time involved to perform well in all areas is immense, and the psychic effort may be increased by social pressures.

Women face, then, the double bind of being a woman: the necessity to prove their femininity (a difficult proposition at best) and to maintain the ability to function in the world as a human being who happens to be a woman. All the possible problems translate into tensions and self-doubt, and only a strong woman can justify to herself all the choices she has made and the way she lives her life. While the women's movement has sharpened the issues, it has not yet achieved the maturity or the consensus necessary to manage the guilt. Short of defying social myths, women have few ways to ameliorate their tensions and frustrations.

The Courtship Fantasy

Romances may serve that function for some women by portraying the one dramatic moment in a woman's life: discovering her true love. The usual word for this period is courtship, but it has a faintly anachronistic flavor. Ellen Moers, writing about Jane Austen in *Literary Women*, suggests a more accurate word.

> Austen's subject is actually marriageship, the cautious investigation of a field of eligible males, the delicate maneuvering to meet them, the refined outpacing of rivals, the subtle circumventing of parental power (his and hers), the careful management at the end of the story, which turns idle flirtation into a firm offer of marriage with a good settlement for life. All this must be carried on in such a way that the heroine maintains her self-respect, her moral dignity, her character as daughter, sister, friend, and neighbor, and her youth; it must be done swiftly, in a year or two, before her bloom fades.[19]

Allowing for the reduction in the number of significant characters in formula romances and for the modernization of cultural mores, Moers could be describing a contemporary romance.

The popularity of romances among a wide range of female readers suggests that marriageship is a central issue in many women's lives, so significant that individual circumstances (age, educational level, occupation, and socioeconomic status) are less critical than we might otherwise assume in understanding the appeal of the fantasy. Women are socialized to believe that a large part of their adult identity derives from the choice of marriage partner normally made in late adolescence or early adulthood. The romance fantasy offers a straightforward and repetitive mechanism through which women can manage and transcend their own life experiences in a crucial moment of development.

Romances reinforce the social myth that this significant event occurs only once for each woman, that each one has a soul mate waiting to be discovered, and that true love develops in an atmosphere of great excitement. When the adventure culminates with a declaration of love, life can be lived as it should be: "happily ever after." No single life experience—for men or women—could be so overwhelmingly simple and valuable, and the inflated expectations for women in the courtship or marriageship experience are doomed from the beginning as less exciting than their promise. In real-life experience, courtship is the prelude to marriage, a new relationship with new roles that confer on a woman some portion of her adult identity. In fantasy, it becomes the vehicle that validates a woman's previous life and ordains her future.

It seems reasonable to conclude that so central an event in the life cycle might carry enhanced expectations for women and that these expectations might be so dramatic in the imagination that actual, mundane life cannot fulfill them. Any choice cuts off alternative choices, and the particular choice made in courtship includes future life situations as part of the package. The complex package is difficult to revoke and can only be altered or rejected with pain and anxiety. If it is revoked, the social mythology of virginity tells women that they can never return to their former state of innocence and potential, even if they do manage to escape from an unsatisfying marriage or love affair. As the old joke says: "You can't be almost a virgin." A mistake made in this crucial moment of a woman's life—or even a decision that leads to a less than exhilarating relationship—may never be entirely overcome. After a woman gives up her virginity, within marriage or before it, her innocence and potential can never be reclaimed. Only recent romances allow redemption from such a mistake.

This social myth for women has the potential to evoke anxiety and dissatisfaction whether a woman is young or old, married or unmarried, working or staying at home. Dissatisfaction with one's chosen mate—or even a vague feeling of missing out on something wonderful—is a natural consequence of the overvaluation of virginity and marriage for women; and the dynamic of romances ameliorates that anxiety by offering a temporary and soothing escape without requiring either a challenge to the myth or a painful life decision. Romances manage for their readers the fantasy of the "all-sufficiency of love" by allowing a vicarious experience in lieu of prospective anxiety or retrospective regret. Focusing on that brief and crucial moment of mate selection, romances evoke in their readers the prospective possibilities of female adulthood, wiping away real-life status to begin the exquisite story once more. They offer a satisfying picture of love relationships to readers, and their assumptions and patterns provide the contours for understanding the social myth and its power.

In all romance formulas the plot dynamic turns on the developing relationship between hero and heroine that culminates in the final declaration of love. A romance heroine may be either single or married; and if she is already a wife, her husband may be Mr. Right or a mistake. She may meet the hero for the first time during the book, or she may have known him earlier. However, the identification of her true love—through the declaration that sets the seal on the relationship—has not taken place, for she has not yet made a final, irrevocable commitment of her emotions. The action of the plot, however elaborated, allows that moment of truth to occur.

Romance plots dramatize the tensions of emotional commitment through an interior drama, rehearsing the relationship in the mind of the heroine as she tries to guess what the hero is thinking, respond appropriately to him based on those guesses, and understand her own feelings so she will be ready to make the proper response when his declaration occurs. The hero does not tip his hand; he waits until he is ready or until he perceives that she is ready. Misunderstandings occur, but they vanish after the declaration of love. The final declaration and acceptance signify the removal of all impediments in a context that suggests that future problems pose no threat to the relationship, for it will provide a secure bulwark against them. Women's romantic tragedies—antiromances and romantic biographies in which lovers are not united—delineate stories of women who fail to achieve romantic happiness, but they support the same underlying assumptions.

Romances reinforce the socialization patterns of women through adherence to a set of beliefs about the way a woman's life *should* develop. If the transition from father to husband is crucial in defining a woman's future, decisions at this stage must be made with serious attention. Marriage must last forever, and women should take the step only after they resolve all questions and doubts. Mistakes are either painful or disastrous because monogamy (at least emotional monogamy) is essential for women. A hasty or unwise commitment may be redeemed in certain circumstances, but it always carries with it a burden of punishment and regret.

The course of a romance is tense and suspenseful, and problems may arise from within the relationship or from outside agencies. If the problems are internal, they can be resolved through the efforts of the lovers themselves. If they are external, a mutual commitment between the lovers can override any difficulty. Because the decision is so crucial, women must consider both emotional and practical factors in making the choice; but romances evade the potential contradictions. A heroine may privately desire a perfect love relationship, but she may not appear too concerned with issues of money and status. At its purest, the courtship fantasy reinforces the belief that love conquers all. Romance heroines may submit to the superiority of the heroes, especially in sexual matters and knowledge of the world, for the heroes have more experience in those areas. However, heroes also learn from heroines, for the power of the female domestic vision of the world to redeem the male from a loveless existence suggests that women also have authority and knowledge necessary for a rich life.

The courtship process requires risk, but its rewards are great. In romances, the most fulfilling moment of a woman's life comes when she knows she has been chosen by the man of her dreams. Poised on the verge of adult identity, between symbolic or actual virginity and adult sexual experience, the heroine of each romance evokes the crucial developmental options for women in culture. The man who chooses her is usually older and more knowledgeable than she; he is established in adulthood, long past his own developmental crisis of mastery. He combines the qualities of a nurturing and protective father (hence his authority) with those of a lover (hence his appeal), easing a woman's transition from father to husband, from the "family of origin" to the "family of orientation."[20] A woman need not fear relinquishing her virginity to such a man or hesitate to define her adult identity through his.

Because this moment seems so important to women, fantasies about it might take on the qualities of a great adventure that can be relinquished only reluctantly—long after the actual transition is completed or the opportunity to experience it irrevocably over. Romances offer a compelling fantasy to their readers because they allow them to imagine, prospectively or retrospectively, the possibilities inherent in that moment of a woman's life when she is a physical or emotional virgin and capable of making good or bad choices. Readers may try on an alternative identity as they read, with each individual book exploring renewed possibilities for error or success.

The predictable repetition of romance reading manages and enhances the tensions of courtship, reinforcing social myths about love and sexuality in contrast to massive evidence that those myths are not true for many women. As male fiction falls into adventure patterns, providing a prospective or retrospective fantasy of mastering the world and controlling the self in new modes, romances offer an analogous vicarious experience to women by recreating their own dramatic moment in new contexts. Although romances may serve as a retreat from the real world, that retreat is not pathological. Romances might be more accurately characterized as a rejuvenating force in the lives of their readers, as suggested by the Hajda and the Yankelovich, Skelly, and White studies. They are less a salve for loneliness than a larger-than-life dramatization of a fundamental stage of life development, a fantasy that fulfills the expectations of courtship or marriageship and reaffirms the validity of monogamous marriage as a goal for women.

In the real world the life cycle of women encompasses many

more stages and activities than those portrayed in romances, but there is little drama or imaginative resonance in fictional depictions of most female activities. Courtship, on the other hand, is both a pivotal point in female development and a process with its own inherent suspense and potential for satisfaction. Romances confront—in a heightened manner—the adventure of courtship, and the very thinness of the plots enhances their appeal because they can be consumed so easily. Repetitive reading of romances substitutes quantity of experience for quality, "cleaning the slate" of life choices made in the past or contemplated in the future and managing the disappointments of women's enhanced expectations about this great adventure in their own lives.

Popular fiction has long served precisely this function in culture. It validates, reassures, and comforts by offering a vicarious world that transforms tensions and resolves problems. But formulas do not directly defy the socialized vision; instead, they offer a fantasy world in which things work out for the best, where the needs of individuals can be recognized and soothed by reaffirmation of deeply held beliefs. A reader does not need to be conscious of her tension and guilt to be relieved when they are, temporarily to be sure, removed. Romances speak indirectly to each of women's roles, most clearly to the issue of successful mate selection but tangentially to the need to perform well in each area of women's traditional activity. And, equally important, romances speak to the need to believe woman's sphere matters in human life.

Romances occur in a world far removed from that of the women who read them; it is more glamorous and more adventurous than everyday life—and substantially more orderly. The world in romances is not unfair; it may be difficult, but it yields to proper action and virtue. In addition, romances depict a world in which it is natural and normal to want a family. Even when the heroine experiences the most exciting adventure, she is also engaged in earning the right to a domestic circle of her own. Any problems that may be encountered by real-life women coping with their socially prescribed roles are minimized by the heroines in these books. Paradoxically, the books provide *escape from* humdrum daily frustrations in a world that ought to be orderly—that ought to provide sure answers to common questions and predictable rewards for good performance—and *escape to* a more exciting and fulfilling world than the reader's own.

The unstable and often unsatisfying nature of women's lives within restricted social roles can be ameliorated by repeated vicarious fictional experiences. The adventure aspect of some romances, providing an exciting fantasy of women in active, competent, and instrumental roles, represents an *escape from* powerlessness, *from* meaninglessness, and *from* lack of self-esteem and identity, giving temporary relief from the exigencies of women's dilemmas. But what readers *escape to* undercuts the vicarious excitement of the adventure, for romances simultaneously reconcile readers to the social myths from which they are trying to obtain relief by reinforcing the cultural message that such roles have meaning and value.

Protagonists in romances are always, at heart, domestic women, concerned with proving their femininity through marriage and family life. Their adventures provide a safe escape that soothes and reassures rather than challenges, maintaining socialized reality by bringing the various yearnings and experiences of women into temporary harmony. Romances cannot provide permanent reconciliation with those roles and dilemmas, however, for the situations are too extreme and the solutions too shallow. Relief is only temporary, because the reality of women's experience in society is so massive that only repeated reading can assuage the felt discontinuities.

The patterns of romances work in accordance with the position of women in society, concentrating primarily on the way men choose women as wives, but including additional issues of female action congruent with socialized and inculcated value patterns. Not all women choose to read romances, and not all women who read them do so for the same reasons. Besides romances, they also have other reality-maintenance techniques that circumvent the exigencies of dogma. Increasingly, women also find methods to challenge cultural prescriptions. Culture changes and old problems become irrelevant as new dilemmas emerge, but social change is neither immediate nor hermetically sealed. It proceeds by fits and starts, producing alterations in the surface conditions of existence while fighting a rearguard action with conservative, comforting tradition.

The meaning of the romance fantasy lies in the welter of competing theories, ideologies, and choices for women in culture. The centrality of the courtship experience has remained a constant, while the other and tangential issues of romances shift. Over time, romances have appealed to many women but not to all. They have dealt with some of women's problems and situations but not with all. They represent one method of working through culturally induced problems—a somewhat self-defeating method, to be sure—but the efficiency with which they perform their function for a wide and heterogeneous audience of women should be unquestioned. Their persistence over time, their flexibility in response to changing social imperatives, and their profitability to authors and publishers provide substantial evidence of their effectiveness and power.

Notes

1. Peter L. Berger and Thomas Luckmann, *The Social Construction of Reality* (Garden City, N.Y.: Doubleday, Anchor, 1966), 23.

2. Eric Klinger, *Structure and Functions of Fantasy* (New York: Wiley-Interscience, 1971), 30–31.

3. Ibid., 31.

4. Ibid.

5. Yankelovich, Skelly, and White, Inc., *Consumer Research Study on Reading and Book Purchasing* (Darien, Conn.: The Group, 1978), 71; Peter H. Mann, *The Romantic Novel: A Survey of Reading Habits* (London: Mills and Boon, 1969), 3; Peter H. Mann, *A New Survey: The Facts About Romantic Fiction* (London: Mills and Boon, 1974), 7.

6. Norman N. Holland, *The Dynamics of Literary Response* (New York: Oxford Univ. Press, 1968), 82.

7. Ibid.

8. Ibid., 75.

9. Christopher Lasch, *Haven in a Heartless World: The Family Besieged* (New York: Basic Books, 1977), 79.

10. Erik H. Erikson, *Identity, Youth, and Crisis* (New York: Norton, 1968), 265.

11. Julia Sherman, *On the Psychology of Women: A Survey of Empirical Studies* (Springfield, Ill.: Charles C. Thomas, 1971), 52.

12. Ibid., 163.

13. Nancy Chodorow, *The Reproduction of Mothering: Psychoanalysis and the Sociology of Gender* (Berkeley: Univ. of California Press, 1978), 142.

14. Ibid., 127.

15. Carol Gilligan, *In a Different Voice: Psychological Theory and Women's Development* (Cambridge: Harvard Univ. Press, 1982), 42.

16. Juanita H. Williams, *Psychology of Women: Behavior in a Biosocial Context*, 2d. ed. (New York: Norton, 1983), 184–85.

17. Matina Horner, "The Motive to Avoid Success and Changing Aspirations of College Women," in *Readings on the Psychology of Women*, ed. Judith M. Bardwick (New York: Harper and Row, 1972), 64.

18. Ibid., 63.

19. Ellen Moers, *Literary Women* (Garden City, N.Y.: Doubleday, 1976), 71.

20. Juliet Mitchell, *Psychoanalysis and Feminism* (New York: Pantheon, 1974), 288.

7

The Limits of Imagination

Men have had every advantage of us in telling their own story. Education has been theirs in so much higher a degree; the pen has been in their hands.

Jane Austen, *Persuasion*

In no area of literature have women writers been subjected to such earnest, constant, and contradictory advice as in the literature of love. Women are the passionate sex, they are always told, and therefore love is their natural subject; but they must not write about it. If they avoid love, that proves they are mere women, inferior to men, next to whom women are always told they are cold, narrow, childish. If they dwell on love they are doing what is expected of the worst of women, who are said to be stupid, sentimental, hysterical creatures incapable of thinking of anything else. And, by the ladies on my left, the radical feminists, they are berated as traitors to their sex, for love is the snare by which women are made the slaves of men.[1]

Ellen Moers, *Literary Women*

Literature is not real life; real life is not a fantasy. But literature derives from everyday experience—and from previous literary works—although the connections may seem oblique and indirect. As Norman Holland says: "The literary work dreams a dream for us."[2] In a work of fiction, the writer's imagination shapes a vision for the reader, transporting her to an alien and unknown world that may appear to resemble her own or may seem far removed from everyday life. When a reader immerses herself in a fictional fantasy, the bounds of the imagined world become temporarily the bounds of her mind. The story becomes an alternate reality constructed in the imagination of the writer but experienced in the mind of the reader.

Because fiction has a potentially profound effect on the reader, it has a special resonance—and a problematic one—for understanding the shape of a culture. Contemporary romance literature represents a significant, although limited, alternative world for women readers. However, romances do not necessarily represent the aspirations of readers, nor should we assume that readers actually desire to experience the fictional world, for readers do not normally confuse the boundaries of their own world with those of the fiction they read. Readers know that all fiction is, in one sense, a fantasy. It posits a made-up world, created by an artist, who may convey a more or less realistic and profound vision of human life.

When we make judgments of quality, we are engaged in judging the power of a novel to connect with and enhance our own experience and our own vision. Readers find in fiction a vicarious examination of lives, problems, and options other than their own. Their individual limitations and personal circumstances are temporarily wiped away and replaced with those of a fictional character whose experience begins, develops, and ends in a different place. But all fiction—serious or popular—is limited by the author's experience and vision, and fiction by women frequently reflects the limitations on female experience in culture. In so doing, women's fiction may offer a measure of the limits of female imagination in patriarchy.

The romance fantasy reflects one part of women's experience through acquiescence to patriarchal definitions of femininity. The image it purveys may be distorted, but it is perceptible. Its problems and solutions inflate the events of women's real lives, obsessively repeating in thousands of books the issues and answers of the female role definition as traditionally ordained. That these books also occur in a world of high adventure, either the interior drama of romantic love or the exotic milieu of suspense, does not change the conclusion. In fact, it supports it, for only by locating these questions in a world of adventure can the old answers and values carry sufficient meaning for the fantasy to satisfy the reader. In the world of romances, the drama concerns the achievement of adult female identity as measured by patriarchal standards: a successful romance, nurturing behavior, and the opportunity to create an attractive setting for a family. These are women's activities, and in romances they constitute women's success against all manner of difficulties. It should be no surprise, then, that romances (with few exceptions) are written by women, published for women, and read by women. Only women in our culture are socialized to believe that love should be all-sufficient and that adult role definitions derive primarily from and depend on human relationships.

Neither literature nor everyday life, however, provides for women—writers or readers—models of behavior that promote the development of *personhood* rather than *womanhood*. Fictional alternatives, like real-life alternatives, are more limited and limiting for women than for men—a condition that frequently shapes novels by women. As Carolyn Heilbrun observes:

Women writers, like successful women in male-dominated professions, have failed to imagine autonomous women characters. With remarkably few exceptions, women writers do not imagine women characters with even the autonomy they themselves have achieved.

. . . .

Woman's most persistent problem has been to discover for herself an identity not limited by custom or defined by attachment to some man.[3]

The great questions of literature, like the great questions of human life, are often gender-specific; and most serious literature tells the story of male aspirations and male experience. The literary canon includes works concerned with how men relate to the natural world, how men relate to each other, how men relate to society, how men relate to themselves. For women, however, literature and life pose another question, an issue they must usually confront before they address other adult choices. And for generations, many women who wrote fiction—serious or popular—have concentrated on that prior question: how women relate to men.

A common and specious argument against feminism concerns female creativity, suggesting that women occupy a secondary sphere in human life because history shows that they are, indeed, inferior. Women are asked, as if the question should end the discussion: Why are there so few great women writers, women artists, women musicians, women achievers? Like all loaded questions, this one defies simple answers because, while it may be superficial on the surface, in reality it requires a complex vision of the artist's creative process. Part of the answer lies in the obvious: our patriarchal culture—the arbiters have been male critics—defines greatness according to a traditional hierarchy of values that excludes woman's sphere. But another—and more significant—part of the answer surely lies in the gender-specific problem that creates for women a barrier to a full and creative life. Too often, the issues of adult female identity must be confronted by women before they are free to address issues the culture defines as profound and significant. The limits of female imagination, in literature as in everyday life, are influenced, if not controlled, by a woman's imperative to come to terms with the conditions imposed by her gender before she may turn to matters that have a privileged place in the cultural dialogue.

The problem of female self-definition may have alternative solutions, and fiction by women has never been monolithic. Writers—male and female—confront the limitations of individual lives from multiple perspectives and offer differing models of experience. Those models may be acquiescent or revolutionary, reassuring or disquieting. A woman does not have to fill all the traditional roles of women during her adult life. She may, in fact, live without any of them. But women's traditional issues—courtship and marriage, nurturing and self-sacrifice, achievement and affiliation—must frequently be confronted and answered one way or another, often before a woman begins to achieve her adult identity. Once confronted, however, the conditions may not remain stable; and their instability induces frustration in everyday life while also offering rich material for women who write fiction.

The profound effect of female roles on all other parts of a woman's life means that maintenance of those roles—wife, mother, homemaker—is a precarious business, fraught with threat and full of tension. Women learn through socialization that their functions include maintaining family ties, preserving romance in their marriages, nurturing their children, making havens of their homes. Femininity has a definition that implies a mixed message. Women perform women's functions, we are told, intuitively. Good mothering, good loving, and good homemaking are innate traits of good women. And failure in woman's sphere implies a judgment, not on the efficacy and value of traditional feminity, but on the individual woman who fails.

Failure is a subtle phenomenon. It afflicts women who have none of the requisite significant others and those who have them all, for the promise of tradition may seem more enchanting in prospect than in reality. In some senses, women may be programmed to fail, for if they wish to reject the guilt induced by failure, they must begin by rejecting social definitions of failure itself. Certainly, some women writers of fiction do confront and reject conventional modes of experience, just as some women write novels in which socially approved models lead to disaster. Edith Wharton, for example, created in Lily Bart a character whose acceptance of her role in society failed her. *The House of Mirth* is a sensitive and tragic portrayal of a woman who could not—as does Elizabeth Bennet, for example—transcend the conditions of a limited and limiting society. It confronts, accurately, the paucity of options for women in a particular social world and condemns social conditions more than the woman who failed. Romances represent a different solution for similar problems, but the conditions from which romance heroines act resemble Lily's problems, and the definitions of failure remain remarkably congruent with her fate.

Many women who write fiction work from similar premises about female experience, and the differences in their fiction result from the same factors that differentiate novels by men: style, skill, depth, honesty, imagination, vision. Fiction by women spans a vast range of human experience, just as does that written by men. And men, too, construct retrogressive fantasies shaped by the conventions of popular formulas that convey unrealistic resolutions of the issues of male experience. Because patriarchy offers few alternative models for female adulthood, some women writers choose to explore the barriers to a fulfilling, multifaceted life, while others take the line of least resistance, accepting prescriptive definitions of womanhood and striving to dramatize them through the prism of the romance formula. Romances—like all popular formulas—reassert the promise of tradition; they demonstrate in a world of the imagination that conventional imperatives and solutions hold true and ameliorate the specific problems of everyday life and the perceived failures of individual women. Readers of popular formulas enter a tacit agreement with authors. "Entertain me," they demand, "but follow the rules." The rules frequently come from other formulaic works, and they allow readers to categorize certain reading experiences as familiar because they have visited that world imaginatively in other books.

Fiction, however, connects with everyday life in another more subtle and significant way: the romance, for example, represents a highly particularistic fantasy which parallels, without reproducing, the limits and problems of real life for millions of women. As readers try on alternative identities through fiction, they experience the illusion of change. Change in individual lives or in society cannot exist without the imagination, without the ability to think, however indirectly, "What if—?" or "Suppose—." But the idea that follows the conditional statement is crucial, for it embodies the possibility of action even when it rarely leads to measurable differences in human behavior. Serious works of fiction may posit alternatives that enlarge the imagination. However, the romance fantasy is retrogressive; it does not promote genuine change or individual growth. Instead, it works as a conservative force, palliating and ameliorating the effects of chaos and change by portraying traditional modes of being and aspiration as more fulfilling and exciting than they may seem in reality.

Readers choose popular formulas voluntarily, but we should not assume that any formulaic world represents the sole vicarious experience of its readers. Most women who read romances also read other kinds of fantasies. Research indicates that people who choose fiction or narrative—books, television, film—for entertainment use more than one medium and participate in more than one kind of fantasy.[4] But in consistently choosing romances, some women readers demonstrate the power of one kind of imaginative world to fulfill and heighten a part of their lives. Because fantasy allows readers to explore topics that may be forbidden or painful, it seems fair to assume that the fantasy world might indicate some of the contours of women's lives by revealing, partially, the limits of their imagination: the possibilities that can be contemplated and those that are difficult to imagine.

Authors may choose to confront social limitations directly, challenging the hegemony of social mythology through novels that dramatize its limits and impact on fictional characters. Romances, on the other hand, work to preserve within the reader's imagination the illusion of choice, to reopen the possibilities of doing it better the next time around, and to maintain received definitions of reality that seem impervious to a direct challenge. No matter how inane, unrealistic, or inartistic the world of romance may be—and that is not at issue here—the reading of romances acts for many women to obviate the imperative to construct alternatives that might lead to threatening change.

All formulas of women's romance share an insistence on the overriding value of heterosexual love. Some formulas may be more directly concerned than others in delineating the shape of those relationships, but all share the values implied by the social imperative to achieve and maintain one love affair to last through each individual life. Monogamy remains both the ideal and the practice of modern Western culture, but the burden of preserving monogamy is unequally distributed. It falls on women more than men, most notably in the persistence of the double standard but also in differing conceptions of male and female roles, the meaning of aging, the nurturing of children, and the gender-specific functions of everyday life. Cultural practice and belief come together in a series of large and problematic practical issues, posed as questions directed consistently to women but rarely to men:

—How can one best contract a fulfilling and lasting marriage?
—What ideals of female beauty attract eligible males?
—Will a woman continue to work after her marriage?
—Will she continue to work after having children?
—How will she complete her housework if she works?
—Who will care for the children if she works?
—What mode of employment—full-time, part-time, interrupted career—will best allow her to fulfill her duties to her family?
—Will "failure" inevitably result from an attempt to combine career and family?
—How will a woman conduct her life as her children grow older?
—How does a woman keep the romance in her marriage?
—How does she keep her husband from straying?
—How does she keep her husband comfortable?

Men may share these concerns, but the questions are posed differently. A man is not asked if he will work after his marriage or when he has children. Instead, he may be asked how he feels about having a working wife or how his wife manages to perform the necessities of child care and housework while holding a job. No one is disconcerted if a husband's job carries more prestige and money than his wife's; but if she appears more successful than her husband, he may become an object of public concern and pity. In everyday life, all these issues are problematic and require individual decisions. Romances, however, simplify them and examine them only covertly by evading their implications.

At base, romances begin with the assumption that every woman wants to find a suitable mate. That premise may lead to numerous alternative plot outlines, but it is not seriously questioned. Few heroines of romances openly seek husbands, for that would be unacceptably aggressive. Women in romances who are avowedly interested in marriage (as an idea or goal) seem crass, scheming, and unworthy. A heroine may not seem to want what every woman should desire because she must wait modestly to be selected by the man of her dreams. Some heroines, in fact, deny their desire to marry at all, but they never mean it. In romances, a heroine is chosen, and the hero's declaration of love constitutes a seal of approval on her life.

The passivity of fictional heroines mirrors the passivity of women in real life; many women also expect to wait for men to confirm that they have passed the test. Women's concern for appearances, expressed through a desire to be beautiful and well dressed, derives from the necessity to attract male attention that will lead to validation of their lives. As Sandra Gilbert and Susan Gubar suggest, the voice that speaks from the mirror to the bad queen in *Snow White* is the voice of patriarchy, represented by the king who confers the approval necessary to the queen's continued status as his chosen wife.[5]

In romances, where pride and deception play important roles in keeping lovers apart, both qualities serve to reinforce women's passive participation in the romantic adventure. A woman who knows she loves the hero hesitates to tell him so until he reveals his love first. Her pride keeps her from appearing too available—and vulnerable—to him, for if she revealed her feelings without knowing his for her, she would open herself to unacceptable consequences. Specifically, she would have little or no defense against his lovemaking. Deception results naturally from pride. If a heroine faces a choice between allowing the hero to believe an untruth about her and letting him know she loves him, she protects herself by remaining silent. Admitting her love without a guarantee that he loves her in return seems unacceptably bold and dangerous. A woman's role in courtship is to say "yes" or "no" at the proper time, a requirement that offers many possibilities for plot outlines. But a heroine must know how to answer when chosen, or she risks making a mistake or missing an opportunity. Those two options for romance heroines hold equal potential for disaster.

But the romance conventions that define relationships between male and female characters represent little that is new in women's experience or in much of their writing. Romances, like many other novels by women, occupy a position in literary culture parallel to the position of women in culture. Women remain on the sidelines of action, where they inhabit a particular and restricted sphere that does not contaminate the social and intellectual discourse reserved as the business of men. And women who write fiction may appear to share a tangential realm in literature, as woman's realm occupies a tangential place in human life. These restrictive conditions may encourage even the most innovative women writers to work through the prior question of women's domestic and sexual relationships as they construct their fiction. Even when women reject the hegemony of socialization, its limits may continue to shape their imaginations, and social mythology undoubtedly influences the ways in which fiction by women has been and continues to be read—or misread.

In the past decade or so, innovative works of feminist criticism have offered new readings of literature that move toward understanding women's writing in the context of a patriarchal culture. Feminist critics have reevaluated literary expression by both men and women, documented the impact of sexist assumptions on writers and critics, reclaimed neglected works by women writers, and challenged literary judgments that deny the female voice an equal role with the male. Feminist criticism, however, has yet to achieve a mature vision of female creativity, for it depends integrally on its source in the contemporary and political women's movement. And feminist criticism—like traditional literary criticism—is biased toward works that are or should be in the canon of high culture. Nevertheless, by acknowledging the role of the female experience as it affects literary discourse, these critics suggest that fiction by women has a validity and authenticity that may differ from that of men. The new feminist criticism also helps to place the romance fantasy in an illuminating context, for the issues of romance also appear—modified, to be sure—in the work of more serious women writers.

Ellen Moers, in *Literary Women*, describes how female authors, relegated to the periphery of culture, learned from each other as they created models for heroines, modes of adventure, and a female literary realism that require a critic to take into account the sex of the writer. Even when women write about men, she suggests, their vision may derive from imaginative structures linked to femininity. In her re-reading of *Frankenstein*, for example, Moers asserts that, for all its connections to other works about men who failed through over-reaching or tampering with forbidden realms, Mary Shelley's story is shaped profoundly by the female experience of pregnancy and birth. Frankenstein created destruction and death while attempting to create life. Specifically, for Mary Shelley, childbirth and death were irrevocably joined in her experience, from the death in childbirth of her mother to the deaths in infancy of most of her children. The power of Shelley's vision of horror relies on her profound understanding of the ambivalence of an elemental female experience.[6]

Similarly, Moers suggests, as does Lillian Robinson, that the special resonance in Jane Austen's portrayal of "marriage-ship" derives from her profound sense of the meaning of marriage in the adult life of a woman in her time. Austen understood, as some of her critics apparently did not, that a good marriage depended partly on its power to provide material security. Other women writers, Moers adds, frequently followed Austen's example in writing about the linkage of money, power, and female social roles. If the limitations of gender are not considered in a reading of Austen and similar writers, she insists, their work will inevitably be misinterpreted.[7]

In her re-reading of *Pride and Prejudice*, Robinson supports Moers's point by evaluating Charlotte Lucas's mercenary marriage to Mr. Collins and by finding Charlotte's choice less reprehensible than conventional critics have assumed. After comparing Charlotte's circumstances to those of other characters in the novel, she comments:

Charlotte is not as bereft of funds as Elizabeth would be should she remain a spinster after Mr. Bennet's death. But there is no social role for her, and Jane Austen makes it quite clear that the material condition of woman involves more than the price tag attached to her dowry and the income that portion, combined with her personal attributes, can win for her. What Charlotte wants that Mr. Collins can provide is an "establishment."[8]

In the context of the romance fantasy, what Charlotte wants is a man who will give her the opportunity to perform the function she has trained for and that she, like many other women, defines as her role. Characters in romances, of course, do not have to make the trade-off faced by Charlotte, because popular formulas offer mechanisms to evade the issues Austen confronted honestly.

Sandra Gilbert and Susan Gubar, in *The Madwoman in the Attic: The Woman Writer and the Nineteenth-Century Literary Imagination*, document the isolation, estrangement, and literary strategies of female writers who fragmented their commitments and resorted to subterfuge in their fiction to avoid antagonizing the male literary establishment. Women's strategies can be both imaginative and effective, but they may isolate women's creations from the sphere where writing matters. Gilbert and Gubar argue that the very metaphors used by men to describe the creative process are phallic; and if the pen is a symbolic penis, women inevitably lack the authority to write and create. Some male critics approach writing by women as if it were, by definition, inauthentic. For example: "Thus Anthony Burgess recently declared that Jane Austen's novels fail because her writing 'lacks a strong male thrust,' and William Gass lamented that literary women 'lack that blood congested genital drive which energizes every great style.' "[9] The criticism seems uncannily reminiscent of the critical contempt heaped on romance writers—and by implication, on their readers.

These studies, and others, show how women who chose authorship had to find a place of their own in the complex of publishing and literary discourse because they were denied full membership in the club. From Jane Austen, writing scathing social satires in the common sitting room, to Charlotte Brontë, concealing her identity under a sexually ambiguous pseudonym (Currer Bell), through Emily Dickinson, retiring to a kind of living death in her father's house, women writers frequently avoided the implications of authorial self-assertion through abnegation and subtle subversion. If these limiting conditions have influenced the work of serious female writers, their impact on women who write formulaic fiction seems even more profound.

A patriarchal culture provides few models for autonomous female adulthood, and women's fiction may appear to acquiesce in the limited options for women's lives. The line, as Elizabeth Fox-Genovese points out, between female popular culture and female high culture remains narrow and almost indistinct. "Rooted in the nineteenth- and early twentieth-century domestic experience of women, female literary culture remains anchored in the problems of female being and consciousness."[10] As a consequence of women's constricted options for adulthood, the range of subjects for their fiction may appear radically small. Women's writing may fail to construct plausible alternative models because the culture fails to incorporate an imaginative structure within which alternatives may develop. Women's writing frequently appears to reorder conventional societal norms for women, whether the author's approach is serious, entertaining, subversive, acquiescent, or threatening, for women share the condition of all outsiders who must break through definitions imposed by the dominant culture before they may find a voice of their own.

The themes of writing by many women mirror the issues of women's lives in culture: powerlessness, submission to male objectification of the female self, security gained through dependence (marriage) instead of autonomy, punishment of self-actualization, and the need to construct a personal and lonely reconciliation with society's demands. The effect of social mythology on some fiction by women has been to constrict not only the subjects women write about but the message their writing conveys. Because female writers may feel they lack the authority to venture into the wider world of humanity, they may confine themselves to woman's sphere and to subjects on which they have so-called expertise—those subjects that are frequently defined as trivial by the (male) culture at large.

For generations, works of fiction by women have been required to pass a special test, analogous to the domestic test imposed on romance heroines. Reviewers and readers alike often prefer that a novel by a woman be appropriate to her sex. Thus, many women write fiction in the context of a classic double bind. Charlotte Brontë's *Jane Eyre* was criticized because it showed so little sensibility that it should have been written by a man. Kate Chopin's *The Awakening* was banned from library shelves as subversive of American womanhood. Alternatively, fiction by women may be praised faintly as an authentic expression by a woman, if it can be categorized as appropriate—usually because it deals with trivial (domestic) concerns. Thus we find some critics—both male and female— complaining that recent fiction by women is obsessed with divorce or holding fiction by writers like Marilyn French and Erica Jong at a slight distance because it fails to meet our expectations for work by women. Is *The Women's Room* inauthentic because of its polemic? Does *Fear of Flying* make us uncomfortable because of Isadora's search for the "zipless fuck?" What do we then make of the polemic of *Native Son* or the obsessive search for sexual fulfillment by protagonists in Philip Roth?

Many women writers write about the female experience— why should they not?—but they do not all portray that experience in the same ways. Although romances depict woman's sphere in limited modes, other women have used the same materials to move beyond stereotype and convention and have invested woman's sphere with resonance and metaphoric power. Jane Austen's fiction may span a narrow range, as did her world. Her triumph lies in her incisive depiction of issues women must still confront—and those issues remain significant for contemporary women writers, although they may invert them. Recent novels by women, for example, may begin with an achieved marriage and work toward escape from constricting circumstances. But even these novels rarely end in triumph, for they must often acknowledge the cultural conditions in which a choice between marriage and autonomy may lead to a solitary self, to loneliness, or to defeat.

Women's fiction, even serious and profound work, rarely achieves the status of work by men, for the literary establishment continues to judge it by reference to the male imagination—and finds it wanting. Edith Wharton's reputation has existed for decades in the shadow of Henry James, as if the authenticity of her work could be denied by charging her with being derivative. Women writers may be condemned for triviality when writing from women's experience and condemned for overreaching if they try to expand their range. In a catch—22 reversal, books in which women aspire may be condemned as unfeminine, shallow, and inauthentic—for the canon of literary culture reflects the assumptions of patriarchy. Women's writing is taught more frequently in college classrooms today than in the past, but work by women may be relegated to women's studies courses or perhaps awarded token status by slipping an odd book or two into a traditional syllabus. The literary canon is chosen, ordained, and perpetuated by a hierarchy of judgments in which male equals human and female equals insignificant. Women who wish to participate, on sufferance, may be expected to deny the authentic voice of their own humanity and write about subjects women know. Writing from female consciousness, however authentic, may represent an acquiescence to second-class status.[11] But women writers cannot win, for their status in literary culture may remain honorary even when they write about human (male) topics.

Over and over again, women write fiction with female protagonists who face traditional and limited female options. From Jane Austen and the Brontës to Edith Wharton, Jean Rhys, Margaret Drabble, Margaret Atwood, Doris Lessing, and Gail Godwin—women writers dramatize the stories of women whose problems derive from their female condition. The subjects differ, but the issues of female identity formation may require that women in fiction confront domestic issues—courtship, nurturing, divorce, marriage, aging, widowhood—even when characters appear to pursue nontraditional lives.

Understandably, some women writers have engaged in self-censorship, voluntarily confining themselves to female subjects and characters in apparent acquiescence to the inevitable—or, like Emily Dickinson, withholding their work from public scrutiny. Throughout the history of female literary discourse, women have been channeled into restricted paths that result in a literary tradition—in both serious and popular fiction—with female characters who may seem most fully alive and most believable when engaged in working out a specific set of problems common to women as opposed to men. Those problems—female identity, choice of marriage partner, achievement of domestic status—are so universal and overwhelming that writers and readers alike find it difficult to imagine a woman free to ignore them, although some female characters, to be sure, reject them.

In romances, the formulaic story confines a heroine to one adventure that must last her for a lifetime. Women who write other kinds of fiction may not succumb to such a narrow vision. But because all women face constricted possibilities and the prospect of a narrow range of options, fiction by women may dramatize traditional modes of female experience even when an author defies or criticizes the female condition. To break through limits to autonomy, many women must first come to terms with the conventional options of their lives, which require female characters in fiction to be situated in their womanhood and categorized according to marital status and family circumstances. Too often, it seems that female characters become so involved in working their way through conventional modes that they fail to move beyond them. Adding to this heavy burden for writers, the hegemony of male literary culture condemns women's stories as trivial and meaningless, even while generations of female readers and writers struggle to imbue them with significance.

In romances as in some other literary works by women, the achievement of the conventional female self *is* the drama. Life beyond that goal lacks relevance in the patriarchy that dismisses women's issues as unworthy of consideration. Because few alternative models exist, women find few acceptable outlets for expression, since any attempt to move beyond woman's sphere may invade the world of serious discourse. Archetypal stories—learned in childhood—reinforce the traditional definitions of female adulthood. The most constricting circumstance for female literary culture is the paucity of approved models for female lives beyond marriage. Fairy tales end with "they lived happily ever after" and thus successfully evade the need to provide a future for their married heroines. After a discussion of *Snow White*, Gilbert and Gubar conclude:

What does the future hold for Snow White, however? When her Prince becomes a King and she becomes a Queen, what will her life be like? Trained to domesticity by her dwarf instructors, will she sit in the window, gazing out on the wild forest of her past, and sigh, and sew, and prick her finger, and conceive a child white as snow, red as blood, black as ebony wood? Surely, fairest of them all, Snow White has exchanged one glass coffin for another, delivered from the prison where the Queen put her only to be imprisoned in the looking glass from which the King's voice speaks daily. There is, after all, no female model for her in this tale except the "good" (dead) mother and her living avatar the "bad" mother. And if Snow White escaped her first glass coffin by her goodness, her passivity, and docility, her only escape from her second glass coffin, the imprisoning mirror, must evidently be through "badness," through plots and stories, duplicitous schemes, wild dreams, fierce fictions, mad impersonations. The cycle of her fate seems inexorable.[12]

Many women writers, from the most serious to the most derivative, write within or against the fairy-tale model, leaving unexamined the issues of the future beyond marriage. Nowhere in Jane Austen, with the possible exception of the Crofts in *Persuasion* and the Gardiners in *Pride and Prejudice*, do we find models for a marriage to which a woman might aspire; and the Crofts and Gardiners are minor characters. Only in the exquisite torture of mate selection and courtship do some heroines appear to come alive, face real choices, and act as fully human characters with a meaningful role to play. Alternatively, stories of women who reject the fairy tale may end not in autonomous fulfillment but in tragedy or disillusionment, a pattern that informs some recent feminist novels. Marilyn French's *The Women's Room*, for example, concerns a woman for whom neither the old answers nor the newer options can lead to a satisfying, fulfilling adult life. The protagonist finds traditional marriage stifling, but when she moves out into a wider world she experiences a different kind of failure, for achieving her personal goals requires her to reject traditional domestic activities.

When women writers—for example, Tillie Olsen in "Tell Me a Riddle," Doris Lessing in *The Summer Before the Dark*, and

Virginia Woolf in *Mrs. Dalloway*—write about the lives of older women, they may choose to dramatize the results of domestic decisions made by their characters years before. Other writers may portray women who have passed the age of courtship (or who do not engage in female activities) as stereotypical or peripheral figures with too little to do. Because older women do not participate naturally in the conventional female drama, they may seem insignificant or become objects of ridicule and contempt. These patterns clearly reveal the imaginative resonance of marriageship in fiction about women, because the decisions made in youth profoundly shape a woman's subsequent options. Female characters may appear to have few important activities or genuine ways to test the female self after the socially accepted choices have been made. F. Scott Fitzgerald's observation that American literature has no second acts also describes many female characters in fiction: they, too, rarely return for a second act (as heroines) after the crucial moments of domestic choice have passed. But romance writers face an additional barrier to acceptance and respect, for they share with serious writers a set of cultural conditions that work to limit female creativity, and they construct dramas that rarely even attempt to break through socially imposed imaginative structures.

Working from female experience in culture, romance writers—like other formulaic authors—construct stories with simple solutions to complex problems. Romances are adolescent dramas that mirror the infantilism of women in a patriarchal culture. No wonder, then, that popular fiction for women consistently portrays heroines in relationships—successful or unsuccessful, fulfilling or painful—with men. But as stories of coming of age, romances are sadly deficient, for their heroines rarely even aspire to autonomy or genuine maturity. The available options lead not to autonomous adulthood but to conventional states of being that lack an imaginative structure for continued adult growth. Too frequently, the most resonant story told by or about a woman remains a story with an inherently unsatisfying ending—so unsatisfying that the story must be told over and over, as if its value had been missed the first time around.

Assertions about the sacred nature of female lives do not ameliorate the inherent mindlessness and triviality of existence within constricted spheres. Cultural imperatives do not alleviate the frustration of having nothing original or important to do, nor do prescriptive beliefs hide from individual women the bitter knowledge of their restricted moral purpose. There is nothing easy about being a man, or indeed about living at all; but imaginatively, through fiction, men are confronted with important things to do and with important moral choices to make that may be denied, in fiction and in life, to women. Romances seem far more acquiescent to patriarchal norms than the writing of women who question the *status quo*, and yet they accurately reflect the circularity and hopelessness of women's attempts to find their identity in humanity rather than in men.

Those who accuse romances of perpetuating female subservience, passivity, and powerlessness forget the paucity of alternative modes for the portrayal of female aspiration. In condemning romances, they ignore the common circumstances of women as writers in a patriarchy and they denigrate the value of female experience in itself. In addition, some critics apparently assume that escape fantasies for women are more trivial and less valid than those for men. Certainly, many romances appear trivial and inauthentic from the perspective of a cultural establishment that trivializes and judges their writers, protagonists, plots, and readers without examining them seriously. Because the central issues of many women's lives may appear to lack resonance or ethical power, few literary works besides romances assert without equivocation that woman's sphere has significance and meaning. Romances are less failed narratives than narratives of failure, and the failure belongs less to writers and readers than to patriarchy's denial of women's right to explicate their own lives.

Romances reflect the culture's failure of imagination about women. Shunted aside as women are shunted aside, these stories flounder and repeat themselves in a never-ending cycle of female adolescent experience, for only in the adventure of being chosen by the man who will care for her can a romance heroine experience her moment of glory. Romances substitute for real choices—how life may be lived from beginning to end—a single choice about how a woman's early life brings her to the point of a single action—or decision—that will determine the course of her remaining years. The romance fantasy may be both trivial and insignificant in the world of art, but it is genuinely tragic in the real world where women must live.

The simplicities of romances, in the end, tell us as much about patriarchy as about their writers and readers. Denied admission to the world at large, some women construct among themselves, through romances, an alternative world imbued with a surface significance far beyond its capacity to fulfill its own promise. The sensation, emotion, and melodrama of romances reflect the incapacity of the formula, in itself, to be profound; but romances are no more unrealistic or degrading than the male formulas—the hard-boiled detective story, the spy story, the Western—that critics define as "valid escape fantasy." If romances—like other popular formulas—fail to be noble and uplifting, they have at least a kind of virtue as a survival tactic. Romance writers and readers seem to be saying to each other: "If we may not participate in the wider world, we will construct a drama in our own. We need not threaten patriarchy, for that in turn threatens us. We may acquiesce—or seem to—in definitions of self that fail to fulfill. But, at least, we can make something of the one story that is left for us to tell."

At its best, that story can be engaging and rich. In the hands of a Jane Austen or a Charlotte Brontë or perhaps a Mary Stewart, the story of a young woman's struggle toward adult identity has a resonance far beyond that of most popular romances. But even in these works, the dilemma of life beyond the fictional ending remains problematic. In Austen, as each heroine begins to gain self-knowledge, to abandon the lies and prejudices of her former self and to make the autonomous decisions of an adult, her hard-won selfhood is sanctified through recognition by a man who can take over from there. Jane Eyre struggles through a life of great hardship, learning to say "no" to unviable and unacceptable alternatives; but she earns for her courage the opportunity to spend the rest of her life caring for Mr. Rochester in his infirmity.

Popular romances offer similar resolutions but rarely aspire to such heights of significance. And yet, their failure to find an alternative ending reflects less on their writers—who, after all, attempt to entertain readers, not change them—than on the failure of a patriarchy to imagine a wider vision of women's lives. Romances acquiesce by dramatizing choices that should result in fulfillment, for a romance heroine's search for identity results in her identification with and through a man. Through romances, women's covert dissatisfactions with their roles are ameliorated not by the creation of new and autonomous models but by the opportunity to perform traditional roles for a man worthy of the effort. The reward for such adolescent choice-making is acceptance into a patriarchal culture that fails to acknowledge either the difficulty or the significance of the struggle and that ruthlessly suppresses female growth beyond that point.

It is no wonder that romances represent a covert and closed circle of authors and readers, who constantly repeat the one clearly acceptable form of adventure for women. At least in the pages of a romance, women experience uncertainty, testing, questions, choice-making, responsibility for their actions, and rewards for virtuous behavior. If women cannot see beyond those pages, then it is the culture that has slammed the door, cutting off vision and aspiration because the price of change may seem too high. Although one cannot draw a direct parallel between literature and life, women in culture face this dilemma no less certainly than do heroines in fiction. Lacking arenas for action in real life, some women turn over and over again to a vicarious experience where a limited form of action may prove acceptable. The attempt to relive and remake significance through vicarious courtship may be pathetic, but no more so than a culture that relegates women as a group to a restricted sphere and confines them there for life. When critics denigrate the one formula of popular literature that tries to invest women's lives with significance, they deny simultaneously the value of woman's sphere.

Romances would not function as they do for their readers if they did not have a dual appeal as "fantasies of competence" and "fantasies of significance," a quality that offers simultaneous adventure and reassurance. As complex fantasies, romances perform the functions of all popular entertainment. They do not challenge the *status quo*; they affirm it. They impose no demands for action; instead, they reduce the need to redefine oneself or to experiment with one's own life. In so doing, they perform for women readers the same functions other fictional formulas provide for men.

Romances share with all formulas of popular fiction their ability to organize a fantasy world in which the perceived chaos of daily life is transmuted by order, significance, and idealization. The way romances impose order on that world, however, gives them their power to move and attract readers. The human experience lacks predictability, and few individuals control their own destinies. Heroes in male formulas assert control over themselves and their precarious world and offer reassurance to readers who identify with a James Bond or a Travis McGee or a Philip Marlowe. Romances similarly portray women who make some progress toward self-control or find the patriarchal culture adequate to the task. Socialized reality is always precarious. Male formulas frequently dramatize the social myth of male mastery and power, while romances show a path to the attainment of domestic status and suggest that the reward is worth the struggle. Traditional roles frequently fail to satisfy. Male formulas and romances alike locate gender-specific activities in a world where they have meaning, purpose, and value.

Male heroes, however—Bond, Sherlock Holmes, Natty Bumppo, Sam Spade—may achieve an archetypal status in culture denied to protagonists of women's fiction. As Elizabeth Fox-Genovese points out:

The dominant themes of female literary culture—female consciousness as shaped by the domestic legacy, female reproductive power, female subordination at home and in the world—run through a range of works otherwise differentiated by genre, style, and seriousness. These same themes, to be sure, make their way into the dominant male literary culture—but objectified, as that from which to escape.[13]

The female literary imagination as elaborated in romances takes its form from the dominant culture and exists in harmony with it, in a submerged and secondary position. It accepts the strictures of social mythology and turns them inside out, not to challenge them but to explore them from a different vantage point. Because romances do not undermine their readers' expectations, they fail to confront the constricting patterns of women's lives. Ironically, the reward for their acquiescence is to ceaselessly repeat and assert values that are taken for granted—and need not be explored—in the dominant culture.

Romances repetitively work out female images created within a patriarchal culture. They are dramas, within defined limits, of women's experience, women's interests, and women's aspirations. As art, they are profoundly unsatisfying and profoundly derivative, for they represent a pathetic attempt to make dramatic a story that seems to lack resonance, to tell a tale that has been prescribed in stereotype and outline, and to make triumphant a climax that annihilates rather than transcends or fulfills. And many women acquiesce in the patriarchal conditions of their story, and in so doing accept the reward of passivity—a reflected self. Tragically, the audience embraces the tale and repeats it desperately, hoping this time to find a way around the inevitable. The most creative romance writers find a new way to tell the old story or find a new kind of heroine who may live out a vicarious romantic adventure for readers. However, if we are finally unsatisfied with the art of romances, it lies in their failure to elaborate mature and triumphant models for female life beyond marriage, motherhood, and femininity, a failure that may also be characteristic of more serious literature about women.

Romance heroines exhibit a profound dichotomy between their apparent potential and their domestic fate. Over and over, heroines are presented as interesting women with courage, spunk, integrity, character, and personality. But their reward for being better fails to compensate them for their superiority. Domestication transforms the threatening part of their behavior (that which is like men or raises them above other women in the story) from being truly challenging. By accepting marriage as the ultimate reward, heroines become rationalized as women.

Because romances capitulate to patriarchal and imposed

norms, it is appropriate that the central male character represents the voice of authority. He must simultaneously approve the heroine and her story by making her his own at the end. Romances carry the message that a woman's behavior may be aggressive or deviant and still be acceptable *if* she is approved by the hero who makes the definitive statement about her life. The life of autonomy for all human beings—male or female—is difficult, for to assert the self is to be judged, and even men find autonomous action threatening. Men, however, are under an imperative to try. For women, however, it may seem easier not to try, for they must succeed twice: once to be taken seriously and once to achieve. Aspiration beyond female definitions may risk the ultimate failure: the loss of femininity. Romances employ a subterfuge that recognizes female assertion within limits that do not let women stray too far.

And yet, within these formulaic limits, romance writers have elaborated innumerable ways to tell a repetitive story. All romances build on the same premises and the same concerns, but the form they take in working out the implications of their premises varies among authors and formulas. Women may not be heroines after they are consigned for life to a mate; but at least before that moment, they may participate in a wide range of dilemmas and experiences. Heroines of romances must work out their destinies in different circumstances and against different odds within a formulaic structure that replays a constricted drama in a wide range of potential conditions. Acting imaginatively on a common experience for women in culture, romance authors acquiesce; but they also insist for their readers that woman's sphere can include adventure, excitement, and significance. Where else can women find vicarious confirmation that qualities they value—love, commitment, nurturing, attachment—actually matter in human experience? Certainly not in female characters in the entertainment media that must appeal to a heterogeneous audience, or in the popular male fantasies, or in serious fiction that challenges woman's sphere.

The romance fantasy reconciles readers to the cultural prescriptions of patriarchy. Undoubtedly, it performs that function effectively. It appears particularly appropriate, if tragic, that romances should be a dominant form of fictional fantasy in a period of enhanced options and rising expectations for women, for women's niche in culture has at least the potential to be comfortable and rewarding. And many women understand that, for them, autonomous choices may have consequences that they find disquieting or unacceptable. If women were permitted the same routes to fulfillment as men, the romance fantasy might become irrelevant to their lives; but must all women—all people?—make the same choices?

The power of the romance fantasy to move and engage its readers derives from its resilience and from its ability to incorporate and manage cultural change within a rich variety of plots. The persistence of the romance fantasy in our time may be no cause for celebration; and yet, the rejuvenating force of formulaic romances in the lives of individual readers need not be feared or denied. The aspects of culture traditionally reserved to women—loving, nurturing, selflessness, and caring—are valuable qualities in human culture. The romance fantasy allows its readers to celebrate those values without apology, and it implies that women also have significant power when romance heroes voluntarily come to recognize the unique authority of women to enrich their lives.

Although the romance fantasy—like all formula work—inevitably fails as a full and challenging model for human life, it succeeds as a tactic for preserving values the culture professes to exalt and covertly devalues. Despite their acquiescence to patriarchy, romances strongly reassert the belief that woman's sphere is more than merely tangential to human life. And in insisting that women also have a part to play in human affairs, romances offer to readers a vicarious drama in which they may be, for once, central to their own stories.

Notes

1. Ellen Moers, *Literary Women* (Garden City, N.Y.: Doubleday, 1976), 143.

2. Norman N. Holland, *The Dynamics of Literary Response* (New York: Oxford Univ. Press, 1968), 75.

3. Carolyn Heilbrun, *Reinventing Womanhood* (New York: Norton, 1979), 71–72.

4. Yankelovich, Skelly, and White, Inc., *Consumer Research Study on Reading and Book Purchasing* (Darien, Conn.: The Group, 1978), 28.

5. Sandra M. Gilbert and Susan Gubar, *The Madwoman in the Attic: The Woman Writer and the Nineteenth-Century Literary Imagination* (New Haven: Yale Univ. Press, 1979), 37–38.

6. Moers, *Literary Women*, 91–99.

7. Ibid., 71–78.

8. Lillian Robinson, *Sex, Class, and Culture* (Bloomington: Indiana Univ. Press, 1978), 188–89.

9. Gilbert and Gubar, *The Madwoman in the Attic*, 9.

10. Elizabeth Fox-Genovese, "The New Female Literary Culture," *The Antioch Review* 38 (Spring 1980): 197.

11. Ibid., 194.

12. Gilbert and Gubar, *The Madwoman in the Attic*, 42.

13. Fox-Genovese, "The New Female Literary Culture," 216.

Bibliography

Selected Romances

The Originals

1741   Samuel Richardson, *Pamela*
1747   Samuel Richardson, *Clarissa Harlowe*
1791   Susanna Haswell Rowson, *Charlotte Temple*
1813   Jane Austen, *Pride and Prejudice*
1816   Jane Austen, *Emma*
1818   Jane Austen, *Northanger Abbey*
1818   Jane Austen, *Persuasion*
1847   Charlotte Brontë, *Jane Eyre*
1847   Emily Brontë, *Wuthering Heights*
1936   Margaret Mitchell, *Gone With the Wind*
1938   Daphne du Maurier, *Rebecca*
1942   Marcia Davenport, *The Valley of Decision*
1944   Kathleen Winsor, *Forever Amber*
1976   Margaret Atwood, *Lady Oracle*

Series Romances

Candlelight Ecstasy Romances (New York: Dell)
   #2—Jayne Castle, *Gentle Pirate* (1980)
   #114—Bonnie Drake, *Lover From the Sea* (1983)
   #13—Sally DuBois, *The Marriage Season* (1981)
   #15—Frances Flores, *Desperate Longings* (1981)
   #1—Amii Lorin, *The Tawny Gold Man* (1980)
   #7—Amii Lorin, *The Game Is Played* (1981)
Candlelight Romances (New York: Dell)
   #636—Jean Hager, *Portrait of Love* (1981)
   #575—Rosalind Welles, *Entwined Destinies* (1980)

Finding Mr. Right (New York: Avon Books)
  Elaine Raco Chase, *Best Laid Plans* (1983)
  Elizabeth Neff Walker, *Paper Tiger* (1983)
Harlequin American Romances (Toronto: Harlequin Books)
  #8—Rayanne Moore, *Thin White Line* (1983)
  #2—Kathleen Gilles Seidel, *The Same Last Name* (1983)
  #5—Jackie Weger, *A Strong and Tender Thread* (1983)
Harlequin Presents (Toronto: Harlequin Books)
  #559—Lindsay Armstrong, *Melt a Frozen Heart* (1983)
  #397—Rosemary Carter, *Desert Dream* (1980)
  #506—Daphne Clair, *The Loving Trap* (1982)
  #561—Sara Craven, *Counterfeit Bride* (1983)
  #192—Janet Dailey, *Fiesta San Antonio* (1977)
  #267—Janet Dailey, *For Bitter or Worse* (1979)
  #391—Janet Dailey, *Heart of Stone* (1980)
  #326—Janet Dailey, *A Land Called Deseret* (1979)
  #124—Janet Dailey, *No Quarter Asked* (1976)
  #399—Janet Dailey, *One of the Boys* (1980)
  #567—Robyn Donald, *Mansion for My Love* (1983)
  #403—Elizabeth Graham, *Thief of Copper Canyon* (1981)
  #447—Flora Kidd, *A Personal Affair* (1981)
  #268—Charlotte Lamb, *Disturbing Stranger* (1979)
  #339—Charlotte Lamb, *Frustration* (1980)
  #412—Charlotte Lamb, *Man's World* (1981)
  #417—Charlotte Lamb, *Stranger in the Night* (1981)
  #402—Anne Mather, *Images of Love* (1980)
  #587—Carole Mortimer, *Hidden Love* (1983)
  #433—Karen van der Zee, *A Secret Sorrow* (1981)
  #544—Karen van der Zee, *Waiting* (1982)
  #395—Anne Weale, *The First Officer* (1980)
  #542—Sally Wentworth, *Semi-Detached Marriage* (1982)
Harlequin Romances (Toronto: Harlequin Books)
  #2017—Katrina Britt, *The Emerald Garden* (1976)
  #2228—Flora Kidd, *The Bargain Bride* (1979)
  #2229—Roumelia Lane, *Hidden Rapture* (1979)
  #2227—Margaret Pargeter, *The Wild Rowan* (1979)
  #2232—Kay Thorpe, *The Wilderness Trail* (1979)
Love and Life (New York: Ballantine)
  #7—Carole Nelson Douglas, *In Her Prime* (1982)
  #18—Fern Michaels, *All She Can Be* (1983)
Loveswept Romances (New York: Bantam)
  #5—Carla Neggers, *Matching Wits* (1983)
  #4—Fayrene Preston, *Silver Miracles* (1983)

Rapture Romances (New York: New American Library)
  #3—Jeanette Ernest, *Lover's Lair* (1982)
  #2—Lisa McConnell, *River of Love* (1982)
Second Chance at Love (New York: Jove)
  #106—Sandra Brown, *Relentless Desire* (1983)
  #76—LaVyrle Spencer, *Forsaking All Others* (1982)
Silhouette Desire (New York: Silhouette Books)
  #38—Billie Douglas, *Sweet Serenity* (1983)
  #25—Stephanie James, *Renaissance Man* (1982)
Silhouette Intimate Moments (New York: Silhouette Books)
  #2—Nora Roberts, *Once More With Feeling* (1983)
  #4—Pat Wallace, *Sweetheart Contract* (1983)
Silhouette Romances (New York: Silhouette Books)
  #30—Diana Dixon, *Return Engagement* (1980)
  #105—Laura Eden, *Mistaken Identity* (1981)
  #184—Laura Hardy, *Dark Fantasy* (1982)
  #67—Brooke Hastings, *Island Conquest* (1981)
  #60—Heather Hill, *Green Paradise* (1981)
  #51—Elizabeth Hunter, *Bride of the Sun* (1980)
  #55—Catherine Ladame, *Winter's Heart* (1981)
  #36—Rena McKay, *The Bridal Trap* (1980)
  #58—Sondra Stanford, *Long Winter's Night* (1981)
  #49—Linda Wisdom, *Dancer in the Shadows* (1980)
Silhouette Special Editions (New York: Silhouette Books)
  #23—Maggi Charles, *Love's Golden Shadow* (1982)
  #1—Janet Dailey, *Terms of Surrender* (1982)
  #87—Diana Dixon, *Jessica: Take Two* (1983)
  #41—Carole Halston, *Collision Course* (1982)
  #49—Brooke Hastings, *A Matter of Time* (1982)
  #21—Brooke Hastings, *Rough Diamond* (1982)

Erotic Historical Romances

Rebecca Brandewyne, *Forever My Love* (New York: Warner, 1982)
Lolah Burford, *Alyx* (New York: Signet, 1977)
Jude Devereaux (New York: Pocket)
  Highland Velvet (1982)
  Velvet Song (1983)
Patricia Gallagher (New York: Avon)
  Castles in the Air (1976)
  No Greater Love (1979)
Rosemary Rogers (New York: Avon)
  Dark Fires (1975)

Lost Love, Last Love (1980)
Sweet Savage Love (1975)
Wicked Loving Lies (1976)
LaVyrle Spencer
   The Fulfillment (New York: Avon, 1979)
   Hummingbird (New York: Jove, 1983)
Kathleen Woodiwiss (New York: Avon)
   Ashes in the Wind (1979)
   The Flame and the Flower (1972)
   A Rose in Winter (1982)
   Shanna (1977)

Erotic Contemporary Romances

Harlequin SuperRomances (Toronto: Worldwide)
   #17—Megan Alexander, *Contract for Marriage* (1982)
   #51—Judith Duncan, *Tender Rhapsody* (1983)
   #2—Willa Lambert, *Love's Emerald Flame* (1980)
   #5—Abra Taylor, *Cloud Over Paradise* (1981)
Janet Dailey (New York: Pocket Books)
   Night Way (1981)
   Ride the Thunder (1980)
   Stands a Calder Man (1983)
   This Calder Sky (1981)
   This Calder Range (1982)
   Touch the Wind (1980)
Danielle Steel (New York: Dell)
   Crossings (1982)
   Loving (1980)
   Now and Forever (1978)
   Once in a Lifetime (1982)
   Palomino (1981)
   Passion's Promise (1976)
   A Perfect Stranger (1982)
   The Promise (1978)
   The Ring (1980)
   Season of Passion (1979)
   To Love Again (1980)

Gothic Romances

Victoria Holt [Eleanor Burford Hibbert] (Greenwich, Conn.: Fawcett Crest)

Bride of Pendorric (1963)
The Judas Kiss (1981)
The King of the Castle (1967)
The Legend of the Seventh Virgin (1964)
Menfreya in the Morning (1966)
Mistress of Mellyn (1960)
Phyllis A. Whitney (Greenwich, Conn.: Fawcett Crest)
Columbella (1966)
Domino (1979)
Hunter's Green (1968)
Listen for the Whisperer (1972)
Lost Island (1970)
Poinciana (1980)
Spindrift (1975)
The Stone Bull (1977)

Romantic Suspense

Evelyn Anthony (New York: Coward McCann)
The Defector (1981)
Mission to Malaspiga (1974)
The Persian Price (1975)
The Tamarind Seed (1971)
Mary Stewart (Greenwich, Conn.: Fawcett Crest)
Airs Above the Ground (1965)
The Gabriel Hounds (1967)
The Ivy Tree (1961)
Madam, Will You Talk? (1955)
The Moonspinners (1962)
My Brother Michael (1959)
Nine Coaches Waiting (1958)
This Rough Magic (1964)
Thunder on the Right (1957)
Touch Not the Cat (1976)
Wildfire at Midnight (1956)

Romantic Biographies

Dorothy Eden, *Never Call It Loving* (Greenwich, Conn.: Fawcett Crest, 1966)
Roberta Gellis, *Knight's Honor* (New York: Curtis Books, 1964)
Rosemary Hawley Jarman, *The King's Grey Mare* (New York: Popular Library, 1973)

Norah Lofts (Greenwich, Conn.: Fawcett Crest)
   Eleanor the Queen (1955)
   The King's Pleasure (1969)
   Lost Queen (1968)
   A Rose for Virtue (1971)
Jean Plaidy [Eleanor Burford Hibbert]
   Goddess of the Green Room (London: Robert Hale, 1971)
   Goldsmith's Wife (New York: Appleton-Century-Crofts, 1950)
   The Haunted Sisters (London: Robert Hale, 1966)
   A Health Unto His Majesty (London: Robert Hale, 1956)
   Indiscretions of the Queen (London: Robert Hale, 1970)
   Murder Most Royal (London: Pan, 1949)
   The Sixth Wife (Greenwich, Conn.: Fawcett Crest, 1953)
   The Thistle and the Rose (New York: G. P. Putnam's Sons, 1963)
Anya Seton
   Devil Water (New York: Avon, 1962)
   Katherine (Greenwich, Conn.: Fawcett Crest, 1954)

Regency Romances

Jane Austen and Another Lady, *Sanditon* (Boston: Houghton Mifflin, 1975)
Barbara Cartland
   The Cruel Count (London: Pan, 1974)
   The Ghost Who Fell in Love and *The Chieftain Without a Heart* (New York: Dutton, 1978)
   A Halo for the Devil (New York: Pyramid, 1972)
   The Innocent Heiress (New York: Pyramid, 1950)
   Love in the Clouds (New York: Dutton, 1979)
   Love to the Rescue (New York: Pyramid, 1967)
   The Ruthless Rake (New York: Bantam, 1974)
Georgette Heyer
   Black Sheep (New York: Bantam, 1967)
   A Civil Contract (New York: Ace, 1961)
   Frederica (New York: Avon, 1965)
   Sylvester, or the Wicked Uncle (New York: Ace, 1957)
   Venetia (New York: Jove, 1958)

Historical Romances (General)

Dorothy Eden, *The Vines of Yarrabee* (Greenwich, Conn.: Fawcett Crest, 1969)
Susan Howatch, *Penmarric* (Greenwich, Conn.: Fawcett Crest, 1971)

Secondary Sources

Abartis, Caesarea. "The Ugly-Pretty, Dull-Bright, Weak-Strong Girl in the Gothic Mansion." *Journal of Popular Culture* (Fall 1979): 257–63.

Bardwick, Judith. *Psychology of Women: A Study of Bio-Cultural Conflicts.* New York: Harper and Row, 1971.

Bardwick, Judith, ed. *Readings on the Psychology of Women.* New York: Harper and Row, 1972.

Barnhart, Helene Schellenberg. *Writing Romance Fiction for Love and Money.* Cincinnati, Ohio: Writer's Digest Books, 1983.

Bart, Pauline. "Depression in Middle-Aged Women." In *Woman in Sexist Society: Studies in Power and Powerlessness,* edited by Vivian Gornick and Barbara K. Moran, 99–117. New York: Basic Books, 1971; New American Library, 1972.

Baym, Nina. *Woman's Fiction: A Guide to Novels by and about Women in America 1820–1870.* Ithaca, N.Y.: Cornell Univ. Press, 1978.

Beer, Gillian. *The Romance.* London: Methuen, 1970.

Bell, Michael Davitt. *Hawthorne and the Historical Romance of New England.* Princeton, N.J.: Princeton Univ. Press, 1971.

Berger, Peter L. and Thomas Luckmann. *The Social Construction of Reality.* Garden City, N.Y.: Doubleday, Anchor, 1966.

Berman, Phyllis. "They Call Us Illegitimate." *Forbes* (6 March 1978): 37–38.

Bernard, Jessie. *Women and the Public Interest: An Essay on Policy and Protest.* Chicago: Aldine, 1971.

———*The Future of Marriage.* New York: World, 1972.

———*The Future of Motherhood.* New York: Dial, 1974.

Bettelheim, Bruno. *The Uses of Enchantment: The Meaning and Importance of Fairy Tales.* New York: Alfred A. Knopf, 1976.

Bird, Caroline. *Born Female: The High Cost of Keeping Women Down.* New York: David McKay, 1968.

Birkhead, Edith. *The Tale of Terror.* New York: E. P. Dutton, 1921; New York: Russell and Russell, 1963.

Bolotin, Susan. "Behind the Best Sellers: Janet Dailey." *New York Times Book Review* (16 August 1981): 26.

Brown, Herbert Ross. *The Sentimental Novel in America 1789–1860.* Durham, N.C.: Duke Univ. Press, 1940; New York: Octagon Books, 1975.

Brown, Peter. "Hollywood Goes Gothic." *Washington Post* (4 January 1981): C1, C5.

Brownmiller, Susan. *Against Our Will: Men, Women and Rape.* New York: Simon and Schuster, 1975.

Campion, Kathleen L. "Intimate Strangers: The Readers, The Writers, and the Experts." *Ms.* (February 1983): 98–99.

Cartland, Barbara. *The Many Facets of Love*. London: W. H. Allen, 1963.

——*Sex and the Teenager*. London: Frederick Muller, Ltd., 1964.

——*I Search for Rainbows*. London: Hutchinson, 1967.

Cawelti, John G. *Adventure, Mystery, and Romance: Formula Stories as Art and Popular Culture*. Chicago: Univ. of Chicago Press, 1976.

Chodorow, Nancy. *The Reproduction of Mothering: Psychoanalysis and the Sociology of Gender*. Berkeley: Univ. of California Press, 1978.

Cloud, Henry. *Barbara Cartland: Crusader in Pink*. New York: Bantam, 1979.

Coad, Oral Sumner. "The Gothic Element in American Literature Before 1835." *Journal of English and Germanic Philology* 24 (January 1925): 72–93.

Cole, John Y. and Carol S. Gold, eds. *Reading in America, 1978*. Washington, D.C.: Library of Congress, 1979.

Cornillon, Susan Koppelman, ed. *Images of Women in Fiction: Feminist Perspectives*. Bowling Green, Ohio: Bowling Green Univ. Popular Press, 1972.

Cowie, Alexander. *The Rise of the American Novel*. 1948. Reprint. New York: American Book Co., 1951.

Dong, Stella. "Queen of Romance Novels Finds Licensing Bonanza." *Publishers Weekly* (17 April 1981): 44–45.

Douglas, Ann. *The Feminization of American Culture*. New York: Alfred A. Knopf, 1978. (See also Ann D. Wood.)

——"Soft-Porn Culture." *New Republic* 183 (30 August 1980): 25–29.

Downing, Scarff. "A Man's View of Romance Novels." *Network* 1 (January 1983): 6–7.

Duffy, Martha. "On the Road to Manderley." *Time* 97 (12 April 1971): 95–96.

Ellis, Albert. "Romantic Love." In *Sex and Human Relationships*, edited by Cecil E. Johnson. Columbus, Ohio: Charles E. Merrill, 1970. Reprinted from *The American Sexual Tragedy*. 2d ed. New York: Lyle Stuart, 1962.

Ellmann, Mary. *Thinking About Women*. New York: Harcourt, Brace, Jovanovich, 1968.

Erikson, Erik. *Identity, Youth, and Crisis*. New York: Norton, 1968.

Escarpit, Robert. *Sociology of Literature*. London: Cass, 1971.

Falk, Kathryn. *How to Write a Romance and Get It Published*. New York: Crown, 1983.

Fiedler, Leslie A. *Love and Death in the American Novel*. New York: Criterion, 1960; Dell, 1966.

Fleenor, Juliann E. ed. *The Female Gothic*. Montreal: Eden Press, 1983.

Fleming, Lee. "True Confessions of a Romance Novelist." *Washington Post Magazine* (5 December 1982): 35–39.

Friedan, Betty. *The Feminine Mystique*. New York: Norton, 1963.

Fox-Genovese, Elizabeth. "The New Female Literary Culture." *The Antioch Review* 38 (Spring 1980):193–217.

————"Scarlett O'Hara: The Southern Lady as New Woman." *American Quarterly* 33 (Fall 1981): 391–411.

Gilbert, Sandra M. and Susan Gubar. *The Madwoman in the Attic: The Woman Writer and the Nineteenth-Century Literary Imagination*. New Haven: Yale Univ. Press, 1979.

Gilligan, Carol. *In a Different Voice: Psychological Theory and Women's Development*. Cambridge: Harvard Univ. Press, 1982.

Gornick, Vivian and Barbara K. Moran, eds. *Woman in Sexist Society: Studies in Power and Powerlessness*. New York: Basic Books, 1971; New American Library, 1972.

Greer, Germaine. *The Female Eunuch*. New York: Bantam, 1970.

Grimsted, David. *Melodrama Unveiled*. Chicago: Univ. of Chicago Press, 1968.

Hackett, Alice Payne and James Henry Burke. *Eighty Years of Best Sellers*. New York: R. R. Bowker, 1977.

Hagen, Ordean A. *Who Done It? A Guide to Detective, Mystery, and Suspense Fiction*. New York: R. R. Bowker, 1969.

Hajda, Jan. "A Time for Reading." *Trans-Action* 4 (June 1967): 45–50.

Hardwick, Elizabeth. *Seduction and Betrayal: Women and Literature*. New York: Random House, 1974.

Harlequin 30th Anniversary 1979. Toronto: Harlequin Books, 1979.

Harper, Ralph. *The World of the Thriller*. Cleveland, Ohio: Case Western Reserve Press, 1969.

Hart, James D. *The Popular Book: A History of America's Literary Taste*. New York: Oxford Univ. Press, 1950; Westport, Conn.: Greenwood Press, 1976.

Harvey, Brett. "Boy Crazy." *Village Voice* (10 February 1982): 48–49.

Hazen, Helen. *Endless Rapture: Rape, Romance, and the Female Imagination*. New York: Scribner's, 1983.

Heilbrun, Carolyn. *Reinventing Womanhood*. New York: Norton, 1979.

Hemmings, F.W.J. "Mary Queen of Hearts." *New Statesman* 70 (5 November 1965): 689–90.

Hofstadter, Beatrice. "Popular Culture and the Romantic Heroine." *American Scholar* (Winter 1960–61): 98–116.

Holland, Norman N. *The Dynamics of Literary Response.* New York: Oxford Univ. Press, 1968.

Horner, Matina. "The Motive to Avoid Success and Changing Aspirations of College Women." In *Readings on the Psychology of Women*, edited by Judith M. Bardwick, 62–67. New York: Harper and Row, 1972.

Horney, Karen. "Inhibited Femininity: Psychoanalytical Contributions to the Problem of Frigidity." In *Feminine Psychology*, edited by Harold Kelman. New York: Norton, 1967.

Janeway, Elizabeth. *Man's World, Woman's Place: A Study in Social Mythology.* New York: Dell, 1971.

Kakutani, Michiko. "New Romance Novels Are Just What Their Readers Ordered." *New York Times* (11 August 1980): C13.

Kelley, Mary. "The Sentimentalists: Promise and Betrayal in the Home." *Signs* 4 (Spring 1979): 434–46.

Klinger, Eric. *The Structure and Functions of Fantasy.* New York: Wiley-Interscience, 1971.

Koch, Donald A. "Introduction." In *Tempest and Sunshine* by Mary Jane Holmes and *The Lamplighter* by Maria Susanna Cummins. New York: Odyssey, 1968.

Lasch, Christopher. *Haven in a Heartless World: The Family Besieged.* New York: Basic Books, 1977.

Lodge, Sally A. "Paperback Top Sellers." *Publishers Weekly* (11 March 1983): 37–43.

Lowery, Marilyn. *How to Write Romance Novels That Sell.* New York: Rawson Associates, 1983.

MacManus, Yvonne. *You Can Write a Romance! And Get It Published!* New York: Pocket, 1983.

McNutt, Dan J. *The Eighteenth-Century Gothic Novel: An Annotated Bibliography of Criticism and Selected Texts.* New York: Garland Publishing Co., 1975.

Mann, Peter H. *The Romantic Novel: A Survey of Reading Habits.* London: Mills and Boon, 1969.

————*A New Survey: The Facts About Romantic Fiction.* London: Mills and Boon, 1974.

Margolies, David. "Mills and Boon: Guilt Without Sex." *Red Letters* 14 (Winter 1982–83): 5–13.

Marx, Linda. "Britain's First Lady of Love, Barbara Cartland, Colors the Colonies Pink." *People* (May 1981): 24–29.

Maryles, Daisy. "Fawcett Launches Romance Imprint With Brand Marketing Techniques." *Publishers Weekly* (3 September 1979): 69–70.

Maryles, Daisy, ed. "S & S to Debut Silhouette With $3-Million Ad Campaign." *Publishers Weekly* (11 April 1980): 51.

Maryles, Daisy and Allene Symons. "Love Springs Eternal: Six New Sensual Romance Lines Coming in '83." *Publishers Weekly* (14 January 1983): 53–58.

Maryles, Daisy and Robert Dahlin, eds. "Romance Fiction: A PW Special Report." *Publishers Weekly* (13 November 1981): 25–64.

Masters, William and Virginia H. Johnson. *The Pleasure Bond: A New Look at Sexuality and Commitment*. Boston: Little, Brown, 1974.

May, Robert. *Sex and Fantasy: Patterns of Male and Female Development*. New York: Norton, 1980.

Mercer, Lindley. "Passion to Write." *Washington Post* (18 April 1983): C5.

"Mirrored in Real Life." *Washington Star* (25 May 1981): A2.

Mitchell, Juliet. *Psychoanalysis and Feminism*. New York: Pantheon, 1974.

Modleski, Tania. *Loving With a Vengeance: Mass-Produced Fantasies for Women*. Hamden, Conn.: Archon, 1982.

Moers, Ellen. *Literary Women*. Garden City, N.Y.: Doubleday, 1976.

Morgan, Marabel. *The Total Woman*. Old Tappan, N.J.: Fleming H. Revell, 1973.

Murray, Michelle. "Genteel Escape Literature." *Washington Post Book World* (18 February 1973): 3.

Mussell, Kay. "Beautiful and Damned: The Sexual Woman in Modern Gothic Fiction." *Journal of Popular Culture* 9 (Summer 1975): 84–89.

———"Gothic Novels." In *Handbook of American Popular Culture*, Vol. 1, edited by M. Thomas Inge, 151–69. Westport, Conn.: Greenwood Press, 1978. Revised for *Concise Histories of American Popular Culture*, edited by M. Thomas Inge. Westport, Conn.: Greenwood Press, 1982.

———"Romantic Fiction." In *Handbook of American Popular Culture*, Vol. 2, edited by M. Thomas Inge, 317–43. Westport, Conn.: Greenwood Press, 1980. Revised for *Concise Histories of American Popular Culture*, edited by M. Thomas Inge. Westport, Conn.: Greenwood Press, 1982.

———*Women's Gothic and Romantic Fiction: A Reference Guide*. Westport, Conn.: Greenwood Press, 1981.

Nelson, Lowry, Jr. "Night Thoughts on the Gothic Novel." *Yale Review* 52 (December 1962): 236–57.

Nelson, Martha, "Sweet Bondage: You and Your Romance Habit." *Ms.* (February 1983): 97–98.

Newquist, Roy. *Counterpoint*. Chicago: Rand-McNally, 1964.

Nye, Russel B. *The Unembarrassed Muse*. New York: Dial Press, 1970.

Oates, Marylouise. "The Ever-Changing Faces of Romance." *Washington Post* (5 July 1981): G1, G8.

O'Toole, Patricia. "Paperback Virgins." *Human Behavior* (February 1979): 62–67.

Papashvily, Helen Waite. *All the Happy Endings*. New York: Harper, 1956; Port Washington, N.Y.: Kennikat, 1972.

Peterson, Clell T. "Spotting the Gothic Novel." *Graduate Student of English* 1 (1957): 14–15.

Petter, Henri. *The Early American Novel*. Columbus, Ohio: Ohio State Univ. Press, 1971.

Radcliffe, Elsa J. *Gothic Novels of the Twentieth Century: An Annotated Bibliography*. Metuchen, N.J.: Scarecrow, 1979.

Radway, Janice. "The Utopian Impulse in Popular Literature: Gothic Romances and 'Feminist' Protest." *American Quarterly* (Summer 1981): 140–62.

Richard, Paul. "Paperbacks: The Super Sell." *Washington Post* (13 August 1976): 1, 3.

Robinson, Lillian S. *Sex, Class, and Culture*. Bloomington: Indiana Univ. Press, 1978.

Russ, Joanna. "What Can a Heroine Do? or Why Women Can't Write." In *Images of Women in Fiction: Feminist Perspectives*, edited by Susan Koppelman Cornillon, 3–20. Bowling Green, Ohio.: Bowling Green Univ. Popular Press, 1972.

————"Somebody's Trying to Kill Me and I Think It's My Husband: The Modern Gothic." *Journal of Popular Culture* (Spring 1973): 666–91.

Sherman, Julia. *On the Psychology of Women: A Survey of Empirical Studies*. Springfield, Ill.: Charles C. Thomas, 1971.

Slater, Philip. *The Pursuit of Loneliness: American Culture at the Breaking Point*. Boston: Beacon Press, 1970.

Smith, Henry Nash. "The Scribbling Women and the Cosmic Success Story." *Critical Inquiry* 1 (September 1974): 47–70.

Smith, Wendy. "Judge Rules Silhouette Cover Too Close to Harlequin's." *Publishers Weekly* (26 September 1980): 44–45.

Stewart, Mary. "Setting and Background in the Novel." *The Writer* 77 (December 1964): 7–9.

————"Teller of Tales." *The Writer* 83 (May 1970): 9–12.

Storch, Charles. "Female Execs Finding Room for Romances, Publisher Finds." *Chicago Tribune* Business section (30 January 1983): 1–2.

Thompson, G. Richard. "Introduction: Gothic Fiction in the Romantic Age: Context and Mode." In *Romantic Gothic Tales 1790–1840*, 1–54. New York: Harper and Row, Perennial Library, 1979.

Thurston, Carol and Barbara Doscher. "Supermarket Erotica: 'Bodice-busters' Put Romantic Myths to Bed." *The Progressive* (April 1982): 49–51.

Utter, Robert Palfrey and Gwendolyn Bridges Needham. *Pamela's Daughters*. New York: Macmillan, 1936; Russell and Russell, 1972.

Varma, Devendra P. *The Gothic Flame*. New York: Russell and Russell, 1957; 1966.

Vinson, James, ed. *Twentieth Century Romance and Gothic Writers*. Detroit: Gale, 1983.

Wallace, Mike. "The Queen of Hearts." Interview with Barbara Cartland. *60 Minutes*. CBS-TV, 3 April 1977.

Watt, Ian. *The Rise of the Novel*. Berkeley: Univ. of California Press, 1957.

Weibel, Kathryn. *Mirror, Mirror: Images of Women Reflected in Popular Culture*. Garden City, N.Y.: Doubleday, Anchor, 1977.

Weisstein, Naomi. "Psychology Constructs the Female." In *Woman in Sexist Society: Studies in Power and Powerlessness*, edited by Vivian Gornick and Barbara K. Moran, 133–46. New York: Basic Books, 1971; New American Library, 1972.

Welter, Barbara. "The Cult of True Womanhood." *American Quarterly* 18 (Summer 1966): 151–74.

West, Katharine. *Chapter of Governesses: A Study of the Governess in English Fiction 1800–1949*. London: Cohen and West, 1949.

Whitney, Phyllis A. "Writing the Gothic Novel." *The Writer* 80 (February 1967): 9–13, 42–43.

Williams, Juanita. *Psychology of Women: Behavior in a Biosocial Context*. 2d ed. New York: Norton, 1983.

Wood, Ann D. "The 'Scribbling Women' and Fanny Fern: Why Women Wrote." *American Quarterly* 23 (Spring 1971): 3–24. (See also Ann Douglas.)

Wood, Leonard A. "Gallup Survey: Nearly 1 in 5 Adult Americans Bought a Book in Early December." *Publishers Weekly* (28 January 1983): 46.

Yankelovich, Skelly, and White, Inc. *Consumer Research Study on Reading and Book Purchasing*. Darien, Conn.: The Group, 1978.

Index

About the Author

KAY MUSSELL is Associate Professor of American Studies at American University. Her previous publications include *Women's Gothic and Romantic Fiction: A Reference Guide* (Greenwood Press, 1981), contributions to the *Handbook of American Popular Culture* (Greenwood Press, 1980) and *The Female Gothic,* and articles in *Journal of Popular Culture* and *Prospects.*